LEVEL

Singapore MATH PRACTICE

Appropriate for Students in GRADE 7

Columbus, Ohio

Frank Schaffer Publications®

This edition published in 2009 in the United States of America by Frank Schaffer Publications. Frank Schaffer Publications is an imprint of School Specialty Publishing.

Send all inquiries to:
Frank Schaffer Publications
8720 Orion Place
Columbus, Ohio 43240-2111

Singapore Math Practice Level 6B

ISBN 0-7682-4006-9

1 2 3 4 5 6 7 8 9 10 GLO 12 11 10 09

INTRODUCTION TO SINGAPORE MATH

Welcome to Singapore Math! The math curriculum in Singapore has been recognized worldwide for its excellence in producing students highly skilled in mathematics. Students in Singapore have ranked at the top in the world in mathematics on the *Trends in International Mathematics and Science Study* (TIMSS) in 1993, 1995, 2003, and 2008. Because of this, Singapore Math has gained in interest and popularity in the United States.

Singapore Math curriculum aims to help students develop the necessary math concepts and process skills for everyday life and to provide students with the ability to formulate, apply, and solve problems. Mathematics in the Singapore Primary (Elementary) Curriculum cover fewer topics but in greater depth. Key math concepts are introduced and built-on to reinforce various mathematical ideas and thinking. Students in Singapore are typically one grade level ahead of students in the United States.

The following pages provide examples of the various math problem types and skill sets taught in Singapore.

At an elementary level, some simple mathematical skills can help students understand mathematical principles. These skills are the counting-on, counting-back, and crossing-out methods. Note that these methods are most useful when the numbers are small.

1. The Counting-On Method

Used for addition of two numbers. Count on in 1s with the help of a picture or number line.

7 + 4 = **11**

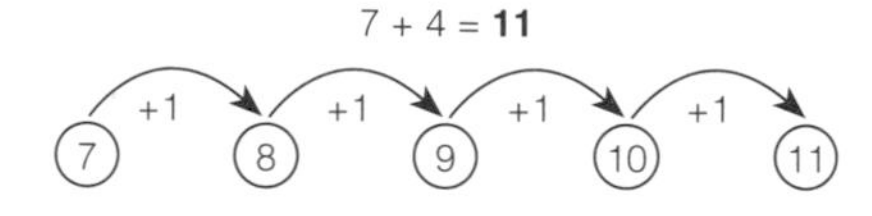

2. The Counting-Back Method

Used for subtraction of two numbers. Count back in 1s with the help of a picture or number line.

16 – 3 = **13**

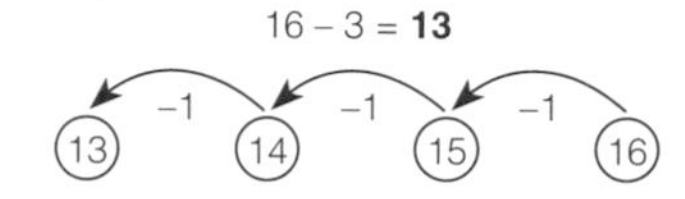

3. The Crossing-Out Method

Used for subtraction of two numbers. Cross out the number of items to be taken away. Count the remaining ones to find the answer.

20 – 12 = **8**

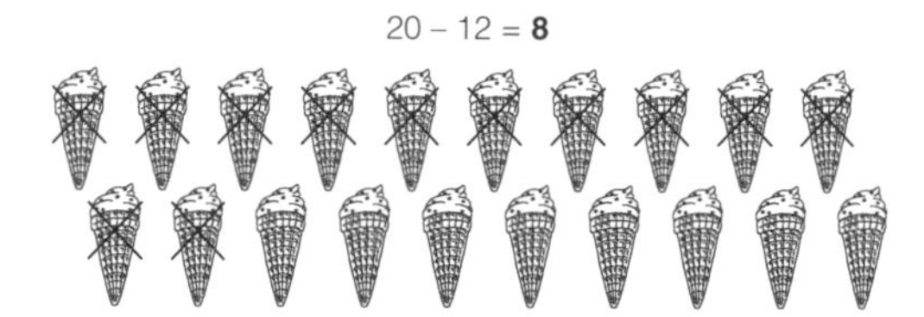

A **number bond** shows the relationship in a simple addition or subtraction problem. The number bond is based on the concept "part-part-whole." This concept is useful in teaching simple addition and subtraction to young children.

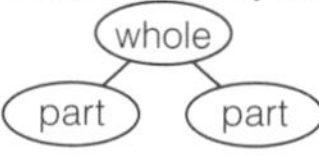

To find a whole, students must add the two parts.
To find a part, students must subtract the other part from the whole.

The different types of number bonds are illustrated below.

1. Number Bond (single digits)

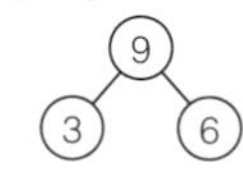

3 (part) + 6 (part) = **9** (whole)

9 (whole) – 3 (part) = **6** (part)

9 (whole) – 6 (part) = **3** (part)

2. Addition Number Bond (single digits)

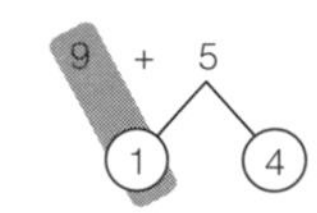

= 9 + 1 + 4
= 10 + 4
= **14**

Make a ten first.

3. Addition Number Bond (double and single digits)

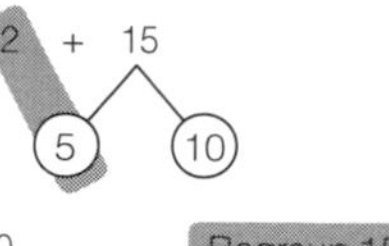

= 2 + 5 + 10
= 7 + 10
= **17**

Regroup 15 into 5 and 10.

4. Subtraction Number Bond (double and single digits)

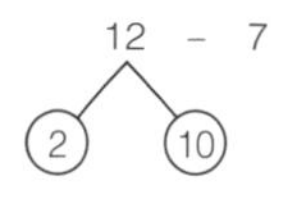

10 – 7 = 3
3 + 2 = **5**

5. Subtraction Number Bond (double digits)

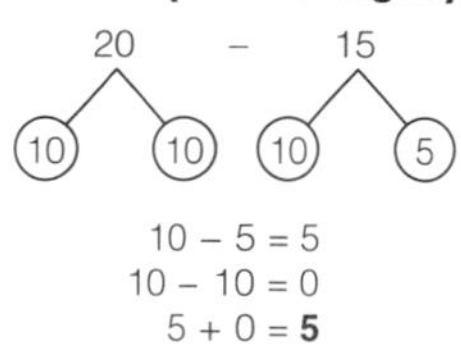

10 – 5 = 5
10 – 10 = 0
5 + 0 = **5**

Students should understand that multiplication is repeated addition and that division is the grouping of all items into equal sets.

1. Repeated Addition (Multiplication)

Mackenzie eats 2 rolls a day. How many rolls does she eat in 5 days?

$2 + 2 + 2 + 2 + 2 = 10$
$5 \times 2 = 10$

She eats **10** rolls in 5 days.

2. The Grouping Method (Division)

Mrs. Lee makes 14 sandwiches. She gives all the sandwiches equally to 7 friends. How many sandwiches does each friend receive?

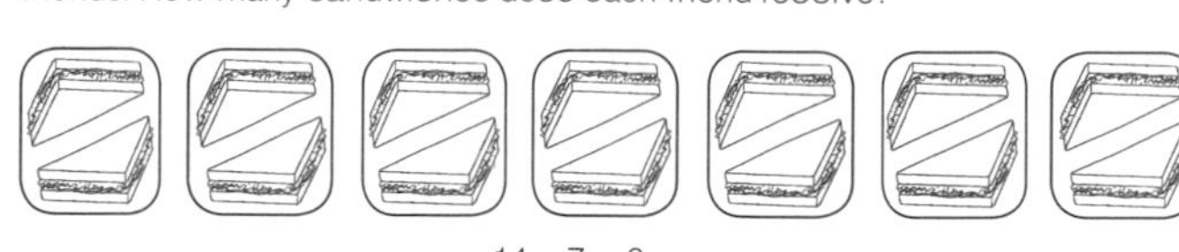

$14 \div 7 = 2$

Each friend receives **2** sandwiches.

One of the basic but essential math skills students should acquire is to perform the 4 operations of whole numbers and fractions. Each of these methods is illustrated below.

1. The Adding-Without-Regrouping Method

$$\begin{array}{rccc} & H & T & O \\ & 3 & 2 & 1 \\ + & 5 & 6 & 8 \\ \hline & \mathbf{8} & \mathbf{8} & \mathbf{9} \end{array}$$

O: Ones
T: Tens
H: Hundreds

Since no regrouping is required, add the digits in each place value accordingly.

2. The Adding-by-Regrouping Method

$$\begin{array}{rccc} & H & T & O \\ & {}^{1}4 & 9 & 2 \\ + & 1 & 5 & 3 \\ \hline & \mathbf{6} & \mathbf{4} & \mathbf{5} \end{array}$$

O: Ones
T: Tens
H: Hundreds

In this example, regroup 14 tens into 1 hundred 4 tens.

3. The Adding-by-Regrouping-Twice Method

```
    H  T  O          O: Ones
   ¹2 ¹8  6          T: Tens
 + 3  6  5           H: Hundreds
 ---------
   6  5  1
```

Regroup twice in this example.
First, regroup 11 ones into 1 ten 1 one.
Second, regroup 15 tens into 1 hundred 5 tens.

4. The Subtracting-Without-Regrouping Method

```
    H  T  O          O: Ones
    7  3  9          T: Tens
 -  3  2  5          H: Hundreds
 ----------
    4  1  4
```

Since no regrouping is required, subtract the digits in each place value accordingly.

5. The Subtracting-by-Regrouping Method

```
    H  T    O         O: Ones
    5  ⁷8  ¹¹1        T: Tens
 -  2  4    7         H: Hundreds
 -------------
    3  3    4
```

In this example, students cannot subtract 7 ones from 1 one. So, regroup the tens and ones. Regroup 8 tens 1 one into 7 tens 11 ones.

6. The Subtracting-by-Regrouping-Twice Method

```
    H   T    O         O: Ones
   ⁷8  ⁹0  ¹⁰0         T: Tens
 -  5   9    3         H: Hundreds
 --------------
    2   0    7
```

In this example, students cannot subtract 3 ones from 0 ones and 9 tens from 0 tens. So, regroup the hundreds, tens, and ones. Regroup 8 hundreds into 7 hundreds 9 tens 10 ones.

7. The Multiplying-Without-Regrouping Method

```
    T  O          O: Ones
    2  4          T: Tens
 ×     2
 -------
    4  8
```

Since no regrouping is required, multiply the digit in each place value by the multiplier accordingly.

8. The Multiplying-With-Regrouping Method

```
     H   T  O        O: Ones
    ¹3  ²4  9        T: Tens
 ×          3        H: Hundreds
 ------------
 1,  0   4  7
```

In this example, regroup 27 ones into 2 tens 7 ones, and 14 tens into 1 hundred 4 tens.

9. The Dividing-Without-Regrouping Method

```
     2 4 1
  2)4 8 2
   -4
   ---
     8
    -8
    ---
       2
      -2
      ---
       0
```

Since no regrouping is required, divide the digit in each place value by the divisor accordingly.

10. The Dividing-With-Regrouping Method

```
     1 6 6
  5)8 3 0
   -5
   ---
    3 3
   -3 0
   -----
      3 0
     -3 0
     -----
        0
```

In this example, regroup 3 hundreds into 30 tens and add 3 tens to make 33 tens. Regroup 3 tens into 30 ones.

11. The Addition-of-Fractions Method

$$\frac{1\times 2}{6\times 2}+\frac{1\times 3}{4\times 3}=\frac{2}{12}+\frac{3}{12}=\mathbf{\frac{5}{12}}$$

Always remember to make the denominators common before adding the fractions.

12. The Subtraction-of-Fractions Method

$$\frac{1\times 5}{2\times 5}-\frac{1\times 2}{5\times 2}=\frac{5}{10}-\frac{2}{10}=\mathbf{\frac{3}{10}}$$

Always remembers to make the denominators common before subtracting the fractions.

13. The Multiplication-of-Fractions Method

$$\frac{\cancel{3}^{1}}{5}\times\frac{1}{\cancel{9}_{3}}=\mathbf{\frac{1}{15}}$$

When the numerator and the denominator have a common multiple, reduce them to their lowest fractions.

14. The Division-of-Fractions Method

$$\frac{7}{9}\div\frac{1}{6}=\frac{7}{\cancel{9}_{3}}\times\frac{\cancel{6}^{2}}{1}=\frac{14}{3}=\mathbf{4\frac{2}{3}}$$

When dividing fractions, first change the division sign (÷) to the multiplication sign (×). Then, switch the numerator and denominator of the fraction on the right hand side. Multiply the fractions in the usual way.

Model drawing is an effective strategy used to solve math word problems. It is a visual representation of the information in word problems using bar units. By drawing the models, students will know of the variables given in the problem, the variables to find, and even the methods used to solve the problem.

Drawing models is also a versatile strategy. It can be applied to simple word problems involving addition, subtraction, multiplication, and division. It can also be applied to word problems related to fractions, decimals, percentage, and ratio.

The use of models also trains students to think in an algebraic manner, which uses symbols for representation.

The different types of bar models used to solve word problems are illustrated below.

1. The model that involves addition

Melissa has 50 blue beads and 20 red beads. How many beads does she have altogether?

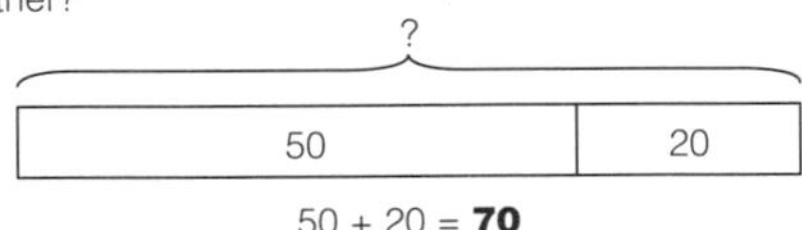

50 + 20 = **70**

2. The model that involves subtraction

Ben and Andy have 90 toy cars. Andy has 60 toy cars. How many toy cars does Ben have?

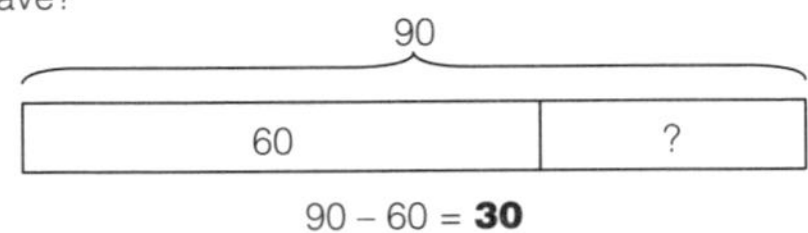

90 – 60 = **30**

3. The model that involves comparison

Mr. Simons has 150 magazines and 110 books in his study. How many more magazines than books does he have?

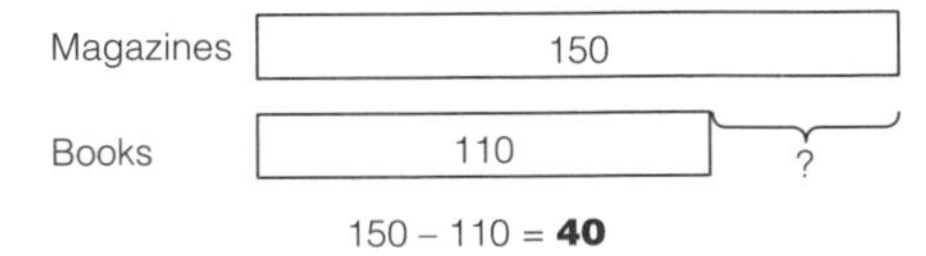

150 – 110 = **40**

4. The model that involves two items with a difference

A pair of shoes costs $109. A leather bag costs $241 more than the pair of shoes. How much is the leather bag?

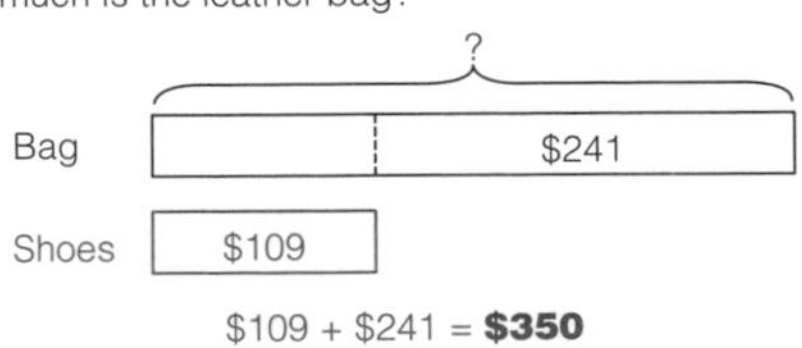

$109 + $241 = **$350**

5. The model that involves multiples

Mrs. Drew buys 12 apples. She buys 3 times as many oranges as apples. She also buys 3 times as many cherries as oranges. How many pieces of fruit does she buy altogether?

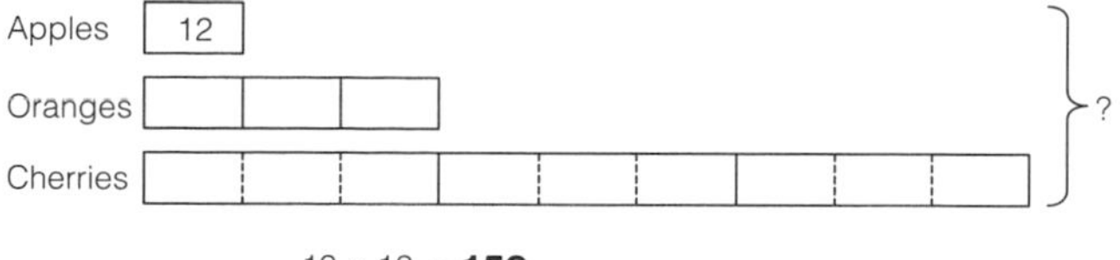

$13 \times 12 =$ **156**

6. The model that involves multiples and difference

There are 15 students in Class A. There are 5 more students in Class B than in Class A. There are 3 times as many students in Class C than in Class A. How many students are there altogether in the three classes?

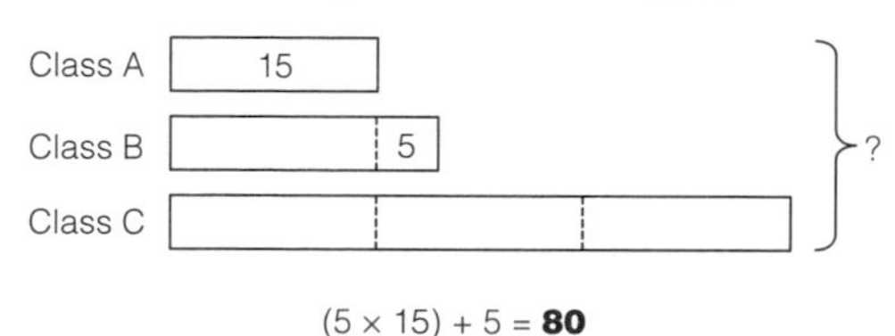

$(5 \times 15) + 5 =$ **80**

7. The model that involves creating a whole

Ellen, Giselle, and Brenda bake 111 muffins. Giselle bakes twice as many muffins as Brenda. Ellen bakes 9 fewer muffins than Giselle. How many muffins does Ellen bake?

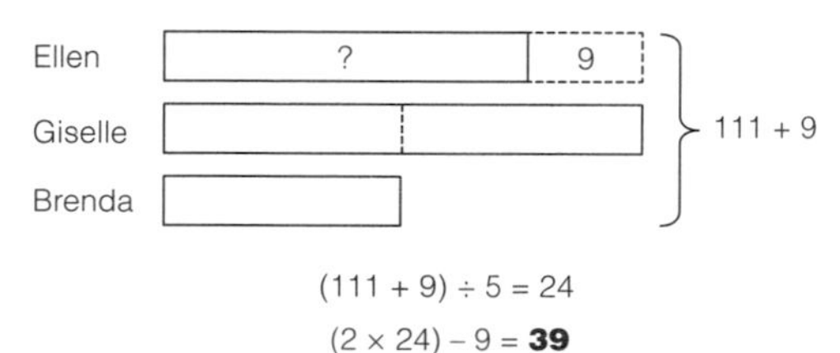

$(111 + 9) \div 5 = 24$

$(2 \times 24) - 9 =$ **39**

8. The model that involves sharing

There are 183 tennis balls in Basket A and 97 tennis balls in Basket B. How many tennis balls must be transferred from Basket A to Basket B so that both baskets contain the same number of tennis balls?

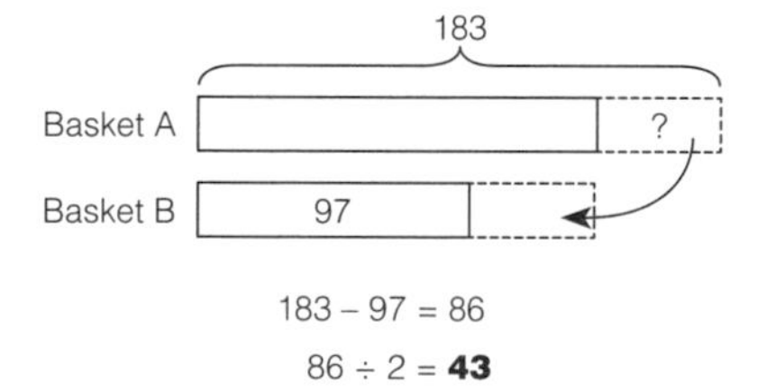

$183 - 97 = 86$

$86 \div 2 =$ **43**

9. The model that involves fractions

George had 355 marbles. He lost $\frac{1}{5}$ of the marbles and gave $\frac{1}{4}$ of the remaining marbles to his brother. How many marbles did he have left?

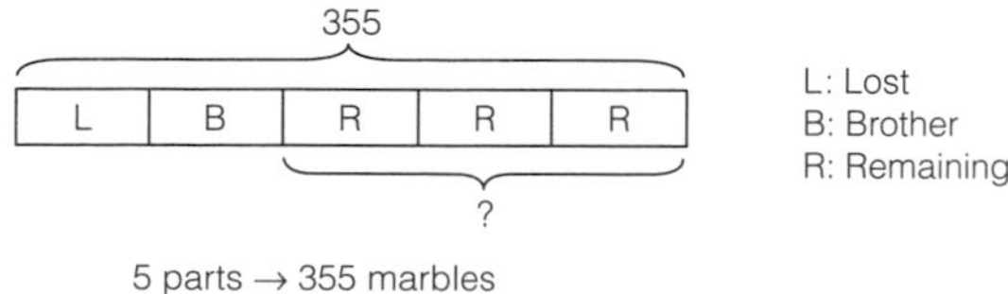

L: Lost
B: Brother
R: Remaining

5 parts → 355 marbles

1 part → $355 \div 5 = 71$ marbles

3 parts → $3 \times 71 =$ **213** marbles

10. The model that involves ratio

Aaron buys a tie and a belt. The prices of the tie and belt are in the ratio 2 : 5. If both items cost $539,

(a) what is the price of the tie?

(b) what is the price of the belt?

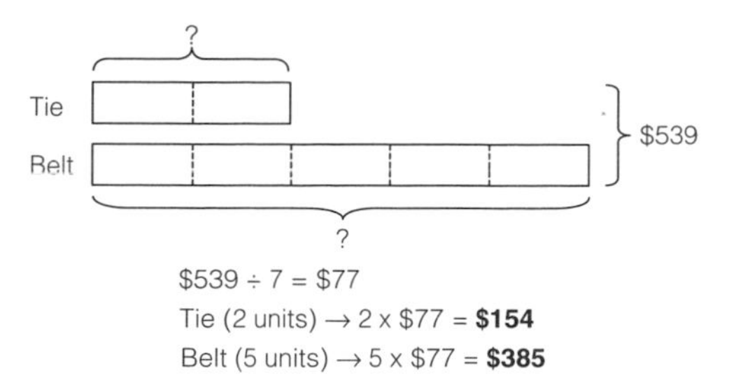

$539 ÷ 7 = $77

Tie (2 units) → 2 x $77 = **$154**

Belt (5 units) → 5 x $77 = **$385**

11. The model that involves comparison of fractions

Jack's height is $\frac{2}{3}$ of Leslie's height. Leslie's height is $\frac{3}{4}$ of Lindsay's height. If Lindsay is 160 cm tall, find Jack's height and Leslie's height.

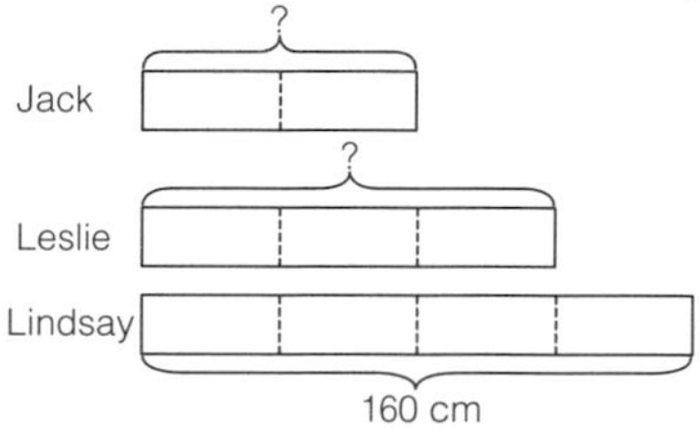

1 unit → $160 \div 4 = 40$ cm

Leslie's height (3 units) → $3 \times 40 =$ **120 cm**

Jack's height (2 units) → $2 \times 40 =$ **80 cm**

Thinking skills and strategies are important in mathematical problem solving. These skills are applied when students think through the math problems to solve them. Below are some commonly used thinking skills and strategies applied in mathematical problem solving.

1. Comparing

Comparing is a form of thinking skill that students can apply to identify similarities and differences.

When comparing numbers, look carefully at each digit before deciding if a number is greater or less than the other. Students might also use a number line for comparison when there are more numbers.

Example:

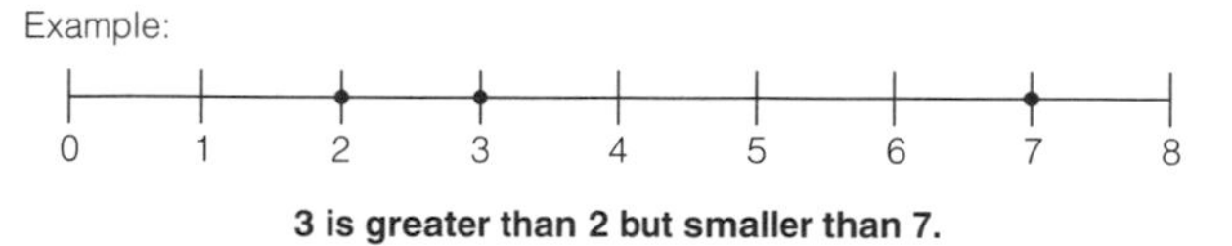

3 is greater than 2 but smaller than 7.

2. Sequencing

A sequence shows the order of a series of numbers. *Sequencing* is a form of thinking skill that requires students to place numbers in a particular order. There are many terms in a sequence. The terms refer to the numbers in a sequence.

To place numbers in a correct order, students must first find a rule that generates the sequence. In a simple math sequence, students can either add or subtract to find the unknown terms in the sequence.

Example: Find the 7th term in the sequence below.

1,	4,	7,	10,	13,	16	?
1st term	2nd term	3rd term	4th term	5th term	6th term	7th term

Step 1: This sequence is in an increasing order.

Step 2: $4 - 1 = 3$ $\quad 7 - 4 = 3$
The difference between two consecutive terms is 3.

Step 3: $16 + 3 = 19$
The 7th term is **19**.

3. Visualization

Visualization is a problem solving strategy that can help students visualize a problem through the use of physical objects. Students will play a more active role in solving the problem by manipulating these objects.

The main advantage of using this strategy is the mobility of information in the process of solving the problem. When students make a wrong step in the process, they can retrace the step without erasing or canceling it.

The other advantage is that this strategy helps develop a better understanding of the problem or solution through visual objects or images. In this way, students will be better able to remember how to solve these types of problems.

Some of the commonly used objects for this strategy are toothpicks, straws, cards, strings, water, sand, pencils, paper, and dice.

4. Look for a Pattern

This strategy requires the use of observational and analytical skills. Students have to observe the given data to find a pattern in order to solve the problem. Math word problems that involve the use of this strategy usually have repeated numbers or patterns.

Example: Find the sum of all the numbers from 1 to 100.

Step 1: Simplify the problem.
Find the sum of 1, 2, 3, 4, 5, 6, 7, 8, 9, and 10.

Step 2: Look for a pattern.
1 + 10 = 11   2 + 9 = 11   3 + 8 = 11
4 + 7 = 11   5 + 6 = 11

Step 3: Describe the pattern.
When finding the sum of 1 to 10, add the first and last numbers to get a result of 11. Then, add the second and second last numbers to get the same result. The pattern continues until all the numbers from 1 to 10 are added. There will be 5 pairs of such results. Since each addition equals 11, the answer is then 5 × 11 = 55.

Step 4: Use the pattern to find the answer.
Since there are 5 pairs in the sum of 1 to 10, there should be (10 × 5 = 50 pairs) in the sum of 1 to 100.

Note that the addition for each pair is not equal to 11 now. The addition for each pair is now (1 + 100 = 101).

50 × 101 = 5050

The sum of all the numbers from 1 to 100 is **5,050**.

5. Working Backward

The strategy of working backward applies only to a specific type of math word problem. These word problems state the end result, and students are required to find the total number. In order to solve these word problems, students have to work backward by thinking through the correct sequence of events. The strategy of working backward allows students to use their logical reasoning and sequencing to find the answers.

Example: Sarah has a piece of ribbon. She cuts the ribbon into 4 equal parts. Each part is then cut into 3 smaller equal parts. If the length of each small part is 35 cm, how long is the piece of ribbon?

3 × 35 = 105 cm
4 × 105 = 420 cm

The piece of ribbon is **420 cm**.

6. The Before-After Concept

The *Before-After* concept lists all the relevant data before and after an event. Students can then compare the differences and eventually solve the problems. Usually, the Before-After concept and the mathematical model go hand in hand to solve math word problems. Note that the Before-After concept can be applied only to a certain type of math word problem, which trains students to think sequentially.

Example: Kelly has 4 times as much money as Joey. After Kelly uses some money to buy a tennis racquet, and Joey uses $30 to buy a pair of pants, Kelly has twice as much money as Joey. If Joey has $98 in the beginning,
(a) how much money does Kelly have in the end?
(b) how much money does Kelly spend on the tennis racquet?

Before

Kelly
Joey $98

After

? ?
Kelly
Joey $30

(a) $98 - $30 = $68
2 × $68 = $136
Kelly has **$136** in the end.

(b) 4 × $98 = $392
$392 – $136 = $256
Kelly spends **$256** on the tennis racquet.

7. Making Supposition

Making supposition is commonly known as "making an assumption." Students can use this strategy to solve certain types of math word problems. Making assumptions will eliminate some possibilities and simplifies the word problems by providing a boundary of values to work within.

Example: Mrs. Jackson bought 100 pieces of candy for all the students in her class. How many pieces of candy would each student receive if there were 25 students in her class?

In the above word problem, assume that each student received the same number of pieces. This eliminates the possibilities that some students would receive more than others due to good behaviour, better results, or any other reason.

8. Representation of Problem

In problem solving, students often use representations in the solutions to show their understanding of the problems. Using representations also allow students to understand the mathematical concepts and relationships as well as to manipulate the information presented in the problems. Examples of representations are diagrams and lists or tables.

Diagrams allow students to consolidate or organize the information given in the problems. By drawing a diagram, students can see the problem clearly and solve it effectively.

A list or table can help students organize information that is useful for analysis. After analyzing, students can then see a pattern, which can be used to solve the problem.

9. Guess and Check

One of the most important and effective problem-solving techniques is *Guess and Check*. It is also known as *Trial and Error*. As the name suggests, students have to guess the answer to a problem and check if that guess is correct. If the guess is wrong, students will make another guess. This will continue until the guess is correct.

It is beneficial to keep a record of all the guesses and checks in a table. In addition, a *Comments* column can be included. This will enable students to analyze their guess (if it is too high or too low) and improve on the next guess. Be careful; this problem-solving technique can be tiresome without systematic or logical guesses.

Example: Jessica had 15 coins. Some of them were 10-cent coins and the rest were 5-cent coins. The total amount added up to $1.25. How many coins of each kind were there?

Use the guess-and-check method.

Number of 10¢ Coins	Value	Number of 5¢ Coins	Value	Total Number of Coins	Total Value
7	7 × 10¢ = 70¢	8	8 × 5¢ = 40¢	7 + 8 = 15	70¢ + 40¢ = 110¢ = $1.10
8	8 × 10¢ = 80¢	7	7 × 5¢ = 35¢	8 + 7 = 15	80¢ + 35¢ = 115¢ = $1.15
10	10 × 10¢ = 100¢	5	5 × 5¢ = 25¢	10 + 5 = 15	100¢ + 25¢ = 125¢ = $1.25

There were **ten** 10-cent coins and **five** 5-cent coins.

10. Restate the Problem

When solving challenging math problems, conventional methods may not be workable. Instead, restating the problem will enable students to see some challenging problems in a different light so that they can better understand them.

The strategy of restating the problem is to "say" the problem in a different and clearer way. However, students have to ensure that the main idea of the problem is not altered.

How do students restate a math problem?

First, read and understand the problem. Gather the given facts and unknowns. Note any condition(s) that have to be satisfied.

Next, restate the problem. Imagine narrating this problem to a friend. Present the given facts, unknown(s), and condition(s). Students may want to write the "revised" problem. Once the "revised" problem is analyzed, students should be able to think of an appropriate strategy to solve it.

11. Simplify the Problem

One of the commonly used strategies in mathematical problem solving is simplification of the problem. When a problem is simplified, it can be "broken down" into two or more smaller parts. Students can then solve the parts systematically to get to the final answer.

Table of Contents

LEARNING OUTCOMES

Unit 7 Rate

Students should be able to

- find rate, time, and distance using the formula.
- find average rate of speed.
- understand and write rate of speed in different units such as km/h, m/min, m/s, cm/s, and mph.
- solve story problems related to rate of speed.

Unit 8 Circles

Students should be able to

- recognize the center, radius, diameter, and circumference of a circle.
- recognize semicircle and quarter circle.
- calculate the circumference and area of a circle using the formula.
- solve story problems related to circles.

Review 1

This review tests students' understanding of Units 7 & 8.

Unit 9 Pie Charts

Students should be able to

- understand and interpret pie charts.
- solve 1-step story problems related to pie charts.

Unit 10 Area and Perimeter

Students should be able to

- calculate the perimeter of a composite figure made up of either rectangles, squares, triangles, circles, semicircles, or quarter circles.
- calculate the area of a composite figure made up of either rectangles, squares, triangles, circles, semicircles, or quarter circles.
- solve story problems related to area and perimeter.

Review 2

This review tests students' understanding of Units 9 & 10.

Unit 11 Volume

Students should be able to

- find the square root and cube root with the use of a calculator.
- calculate the volume of solids.
- find the edge of a cube/cubical tank given its volume.
- find one dimension of a cuboid/rectangular tank given its volume and the other dimension.
- find the height of a cuboid/rectangular tank given its volume and base area.
- find the area of a face of a cuboid/rectangular tank given its volume and one dimension.
- calculate the volume of water in a cubical/rectangular container.
- calculate the height of water level in a cubical/rectangular container.
- solve story problems related to volume.

Unit 12 Challenging Word Problems

Students should be able to

- solve story problems related to whole numbers, fractions, decimals, ratio, percentage, and rate of speed.

Review 3

This review tests students' understanding of Units 11 & 12.

Final Review

This review is an excellent assessment of students' understanding of all the topics learned in this series.

FORMULA SHEET

Unit 7 Rate

Distance = Rate × Time

Time = Distance ÷ Rate

Rate = Distance ÷ Time

Average Rate = Total distance ÷ Total time

Unit 8 Circles

Types of circles	Diagram
circle	
half circle / semicircle	
quarter circle / quadrant	

In this circle,

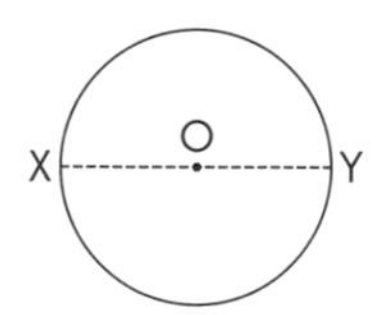

O is the **center** of the circle.

XY is the **diameter** of the circle.

OX is the **radius** of the circle.

OX and OY are the radii of the circle.

Circumference

Circumference is also known as the perimeter. It is the outline of a circle.

Diameter

Diameter of a circle is a straight line that extends from one point along the circumference to another point. It will pass through the center of the circle.

diameter = 2 × radius

Examples: XY = 2 × OX or XY = 2 × OY

Radius

Radius of a circle is a straight line that extends from the center to any point along the circumference. All radii of a circle are equal.

Example: OX = OY

Finding the circumference of a circle

Circumference = πd or $2\pi r$

where $\pi = \frac{22}{7}$ or 3.14, d is diameter, and r is radius.

Finding the circumference of a semicircle

Circumference = $\frac{\pi d}{2}$ or $\frac{2\pi r}{2}$

where $\pi = \frac{22}{7}$ or 3.14, d is diameter, and r is radius.

Finding the circumference of a quadrant

Circumference = $\frac{\pi d}{4}$ or $\frac{2\pi r}{4}$

where $\pi = \frac{22}{7}$ or 3.14, d is diameter, and r is radius.

Finding the area of a circle

Area = πr^2

where $\pi = \frac{22}{7}$ or 3.14 and r is radius.

Finding the area of a semicircle

Area = $\frac{\pi r^2}{2}$

where $\pi = \frac{22}{7}$ or 3.14 and r is radius.

Finding the area of a quadrant

Area = $\frac{\pi r^2}{4}$

where $\pi = \frac{22}{7}$ or 3.14 and r is radius.

Unit 9 Pie Charts

Pie charts are pictorial graphs that organize information. Pie charts use a circle as a representation of a whole or 100%. In the circle, there are different segments. Each segment represents a fraction or percentage of the total quantity.

Gather information from a pie chart and use it to answer questions.

Example:

The pie chart below represents the number of students who like different types of fast food.

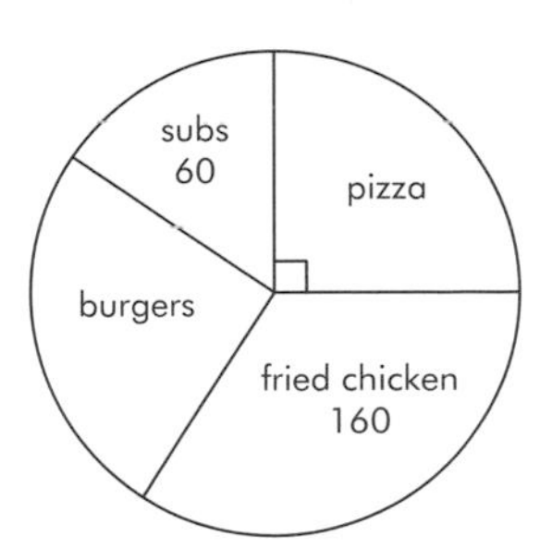

Unit 10 Area and Perimeter

Figure	Perimeter	Units of measurement	Area	Units of measurement
circle	πd or $2\pi r$ $\pi = \frac{22}{7}$ or 3.14 d is diameter r is radius	cm, m, in., ft., yd.	πr^2 $\pi = \frac{22}{7}$ or 3.14 r is radius	cm^2, m^2, $in.^2$, $ft.^2$, $yd.^2$
semicircle	$\frac{\pi d}{2}$ or $\frac{2\pi r}{2}$ $\pi = \frac{22}{7}$ or 3.14 d is diameter r is radius	cm, m, in., ft., yd.	$\frac{\pi r^2}{2}$ $\pi = \frac{22}{7}$ or 3.14 r is radius	cm^2, m^2, $in.^2$, $ft.^2$, $yd.^2$
quadrant	$\frac{\pi d}{4}$ or $\frac{2\pi r}{4}$ $\pi = \frac{22}{7}$ or 3.14 d is diameter r is radius	cm, m, in., ft., yd.	$\frac{\pi r^2}{4}$ $\pi = \frac{22}{7}$ or 3.14 r is radius	cm^2, m^2, $in.^2$, $ft.^2$, $yd.^2$
square	$4 \times L$ L is length	cm, m, in., ft., yd.	$L \times L$ L is length	cm^2, m^2, $in.^2$, $ft.^2$, $yd.^2$
rectangle	$2 \times W + 2 \times L$ L is length W is width	cm, m, in., ft., yd.	$L \times B$ L is length W is width	cm^2, m^2, $in.^2$, $ft.^2$, $yd.^2$
triangle	Add the three sides of a triangle.	cm, m, in., ft., yd.	$\frac{1}{2} \times B + H$ B is base H is height	cm^2, m^2, $in.^2$, $ft.^2$, $yd.^2$

Unit 11 Volume

Square root is a number when it is multiplied by itself to get another number.

Symbol: $\sqrt[2]{}$

Example: Find the square root of 25.

$\sqrt[2]{25} = 5$

Cube root is a number when it is multiplied by itself twice to get another number.

Symbol: $\sqrt[3]{}$

Example: Find the cube root of 8.

$\sqrt[3]{8} = 2$

Volume and Capacity

Volume of a solid is the amount of space in it.

Capacity of a solid is the amount of liquid that it can hold completely.

Units of measurement: cm^3, m^3, $in.^3$

1 L = 1,000 cm^3

Cube

Volume of a cube = Edge × Edge × Edge

Edge of a cube = $\sqrt[3]{\text{Volume}}$

Rectangular Prism

Volume of a rectangular prism = Length × Width × Height

Length of a rectangular prism = $\frac{\text{Volume}}{\text{Width} \times \text{Height}}$

Width of a rectangular prism = $\frac{\text{Volume}}{\text{Length} \times \text{Height}}$

Height of a rectangular prism = $\frac{\text{Volume}}{\text{Length} \times \text{Width}}$

Base area = Length × Width = $\frac{\text{Volume}}{\text{Height}}$

Height of water level = $\frac{\text{Volume}}{\text{Base area}}$

Capacity of a container = Length × Width × Height

Note that the height refers to height of the container.

Amount of water needed to fill the container completely = Capacity – Volume of water in the container

Time taken to fill an empty container completely

$= \frac{\text{Capacity}}{\text{rate of water flow}}$

Unit 12 Challenging Word Problems

When attempting a challenging word problem,

① read the word problem carefully to gain a better understanding.

② analyze the word problem and come up with a plan.

③ use one or more of the following strategies to solve the word problem.

- draw a model/diagram
- make a list
- use an equation
- guess and check
- look for pattern(s)
- make supposition(s)
- act it out
- work backward
- before-after approach
- restate the problem
- simplify the problem

④ After obtaining the answer, apply it to the question to check for reasonableness of answer.

⑤ If the answer is not reasonable, go back to the first step again.

UNIT 7: RATE

Examples:

1. Kevin jogs at a rate of speed of 120 yd. per min. for 10 minutes. Find the distance that he has jogged.

   Distance = Rate × Time
   = 120 × 10
   = 1,200 yd.

   He has jogged **1,200 yd**.

2. Betsy takes 5 minutes to walk to her grandmother's house which is 585 m away from her house. She takes 4 minutes to walk back to her house using the same route. Find her average rate of speed.

   Average rate of speed = Total distance ÷ Total time
   = (585 + 585) ÷ (5 + 4)
   = 130 m/min

   Her average rate speed is **130 m/min**.

Fill in each blank with the correct answer.

1. Rob runs 550 yd. in one minute. How fast does he run? __________

2. Lorraine swims 1 m in one second. At what rate does she swim? __________

3. Mindy rides her bicycle at a rate of speed of 6 km/h. How far does she cycle in an hour?

   ____

4. Grandmother walks at a rate of speed of 1 ft. per sec. to the community center. How far does she walk in a second?

____

5. Mrs. Adams drives at a rate of speed of 60 mph (miles per hour). How far does she drive in an hour?

____

6. An ant crawls at a rate of speed of 2 cm/s. How far does it crawl in a second? ______________

Fill in each box with the correct answer. You may use a calculator whenever you see **.**

	Time	Distance	Rate
7.	2 hr.	194 mi.	
8.	30 min.		116 m/min.
9.		50 ft.	10 ft. per sec.
10.	60 hr.	1,560 mi.	
11.		336 m	8 m/min.
12.	2 sec.		14 cm/sec.
13.	19 hr.	988 mi.	
14.		1,829 m	59 m/sec.
15.	67 min.		99 m/min.
16.	48 sec.	768 ft.	

Find the average rate of speed.

17.

Distance	32 ft.	48 ft.
Time	9 min.	7 min.
Average rate of speed		

18.

Distance	372 cm	243 cm
Time	8 sec.	7 sec.
Average rate of speed		

19.

Distance	150 mi.	630 mi.	240 mi.
Time	11 min.	30 min.	19 min.
Average rate of speed			

20.

Distance	461 ft.	239 ft.	1250 ft.
Time	18 min.	7 min.	35 min.
Average rate of speed			

21.

Distance	603 km	894 km	375 km
Time	21 min.	18 min.	9 min.
Average rate of speed			

Write your answers on the lines.

22. A car travels at a rate of speed of 55 mph. How far can it travel in 4 hours?

____

23. A train traveled at a rate of speed of 64 mph. How long did it take to travel a distance of 416 mi.?

____

24. Becky walks for 20 minutes to her school that is 580 m away from her house. She walks back to her house using the same route at a rate of speed of 20 m/min. What is Becky's average rate of speed?

____

25. Marcus took $1\frac{1}{2}$ hours to drive to his office. His office was 75 mi. away from his house. Find his driving speed.

____

26. A bus travels from Point A to Point B at a rate of speed of 75 km/h for $4\frac{4}{5}$ hours. How far is Point A from Point B?

____

27. An airplane traveled the first 96 mi. of a flight at an average rate of speed of 16 miles per minute. It then traveled another 18 minutes at a rate of speed of 12 miles per minute. Find the average rate of speed of the airplane for the whole flight.

____

28. An arrow can travel at a rate of speed of 186 m/s. How long does it take for the arrow to travel a distance of 2,046 m?

____

29. Tiffany spent 24 minutes traveling from Point A to Point B at a rate of speed of 60 mph. How far was Point A from Point B?

____

30. A golf ball rolls at a rate of speed of 8 m/s for 12 seconds. Mandy hits the golf ball and it rolls for 16 seconds at a rate of speed of 12 m/s. What is the total distance traveled by the golf ball?

____

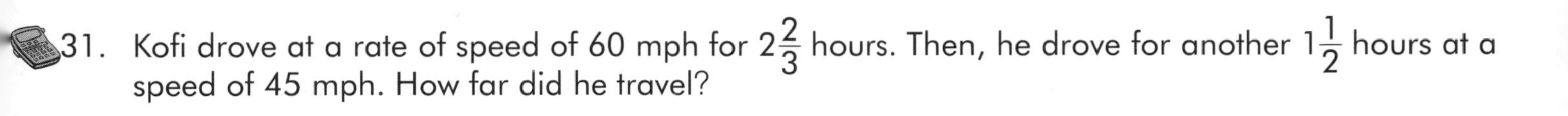

31. Kofi drove at a rate of speed of 60 mph for $2\frac{2}{3}$ hours. Then, he drove for another $1\frac{1}{2}$ hours at a speed of 45 mph. How far did he travel?

____

Solve the following story problems. Show your work in the space below.

32. The distance around a field is 540 m. Ruth runs around the field 8 times in half an hour. What is her average rate of speed? Write your answer in m/min.

33. The distance from Chicago to St. Louis is 300 mi. Sam drives from Chicago to St. Louis at an average rate of speed of 60 mph. If he starts his trip at 10:45 A.M., at what time will he reach St. Louis?

34. Mr. Suksod drives from his house to the office at a rate of speed of 82 km/h in 15 minutes. Mr. Taylor, whose house is as far from the office as Mr. Suksod's, drives for 10 minutes to reach the same office. What is the difference in the rate of speed that they drive?

35. Eileen ran at a rate of speed of 4.8 km/h to complete a 4-km run. Sally ran at a rate of speed of 6 km/h to complete the same distance. How much longer did Eileen take to complete her run than Sally? Write your answer in minutes.

36. Dennis set off from Town A at 10 A.M., driving at an average rate of speed of 52 mph. He reached Town B at 2 P.M. If William set off 1 hour 25 minutes earlier than Dennis and took the same route at an average rate of speed of 40 mph., at what time would William reach Town B?

37. Tracy took $2\frac{1}{3}$ hours to travel $\frac{4}{9}$ of the distance between Town X and Town Y at an average rate of speed of 72 km/h. What was Jessica's average rate of speed if she took $4\frac{1}{5}$ hours to travel from Town X to Town Y?

38. Tara usually leaves her house at 8:20 A.M., driving at an average rate of speed of 42 mph to reach her office at 9 A.M. What should Tara's average rate of speed be if she leaves home 5 minutes later than usual but wants to reach her office at the same time?

39. A motorcyclist and a motorist left Town Y and Town Z at the same time respectively. The motorcyclist drove at an average rate of speed of 98 km/h, and the motorist drove at an average rate of speed of 82 km/h. They passed each other 1 hour 18 minutes later.

(a) What was the distance between Town Y and Town Z?

(b) How much farther did the motorist have to travel in order to reach Town Y?

40. Ricky took 4 hours and 30 minutes to travel from Town P to Town Q at an average rate of speed of 60 mph. $2\frac{1}{2}$ hours after setting off, Ricky stopped for a rest. He continued the driving after 30 minutes. How far was Town P from Town Q?

41. Kumiko left Hillview at 4:20 P.M., traveling towards Beach Town which was 600 km away at an average speed of 108 km/h. Claudia left Hillview at 5 P.M., traveling at an average rate of speed of 124 km/h.

(a) How long did Claudia take to catch up with Kumiko?

(b) How far away were they from Beach Town when Claudia caught up with Kumiko?

UNIT 8: CIRCLES

Examples:

1. Find the circumference of a circle whose radius is 21 in. (Use $\pi = \frac{22}{7}$)

   Diameter = 2 × Radius = 2 × 21 = 42 in.

   $$\text{Circumference} = \pi \times \text{Diameter}$$
   $$= \frac{22}{7} \times 42$$
   $$= 132 \text{ in.}$$

   The circumference of the circle is **132 in.**

2. Find the area of a quadrant whose diameter is 60 cm. (Use $\pi = 3.14$)

   Radius = 60 ÷ 2 = 30 cm

   $$\text{Area of a quadrant} = \frac{\pi \times \text{Radius} \times \text{Radius}}{4}$$
   $$= \frac{3.14 \times 30 \times 30}{4}$$
   $$= 706.5 \text{ cm}^2$$

   The area of the quadrant is **706.5 cm²**.

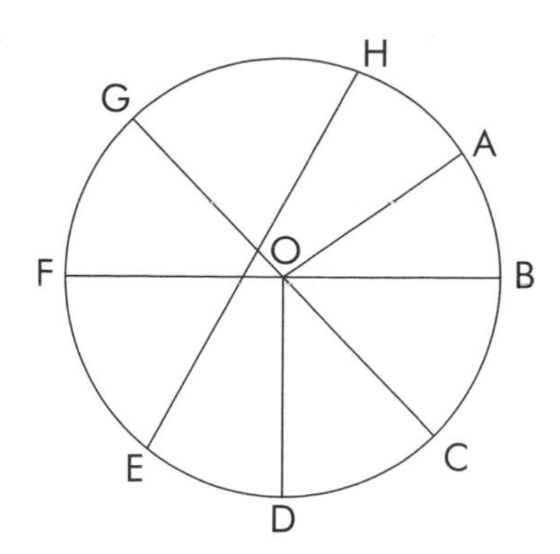

1. Identify the point that shows the center of the circle. __________

2. Identify all the radii of the circle. __________

3. Identify all the diameters of the circle. __________

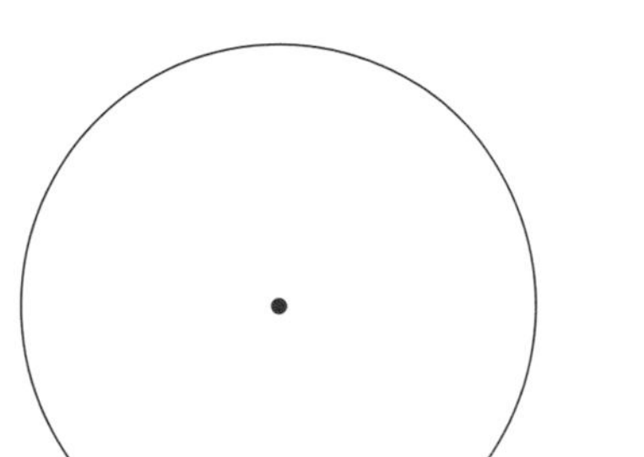

4. In the above circle, draw dotted lines to show a
   (a) quarter circle.
   (b) semicircle.

Calculate the circumference of each circle shown below. (Use $\pi = \frac{22}{7}$)

5.

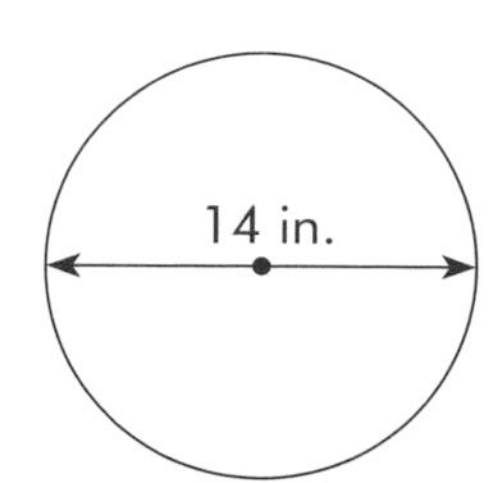

Diameter = ______ in.

Circumference =

6.

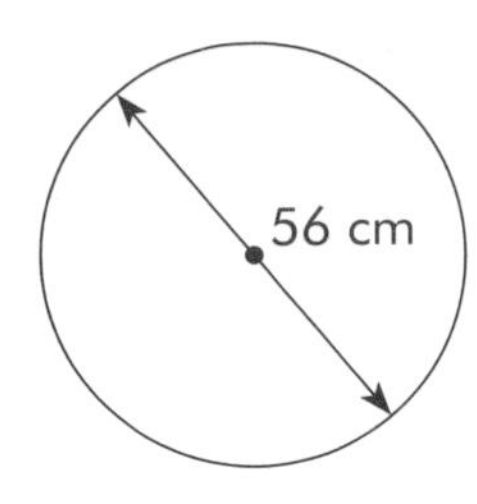

Diameter = _____ cm

Circumference =

7.

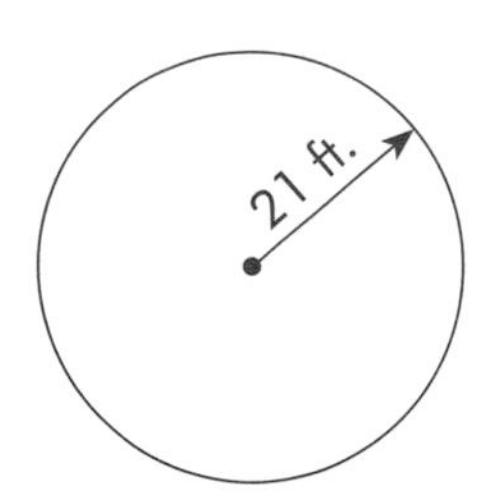

Diameter = _____ ft.

Circumference =

Calculate the circumference of each circle shown below. (Use $\pi = 3.14$)
You may use a calculator whenever you see [calculator icon].

8.

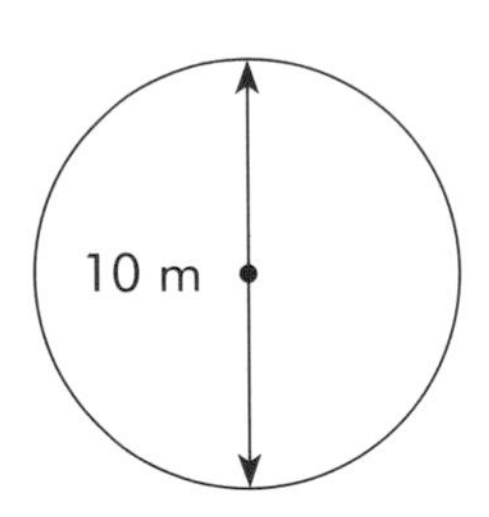

Radius = _____ m

Circumference =

9.

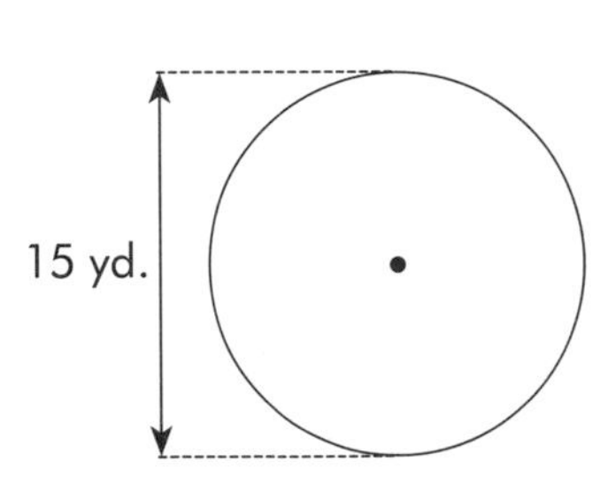

Radius = _____ yd.

Circumference =

10.

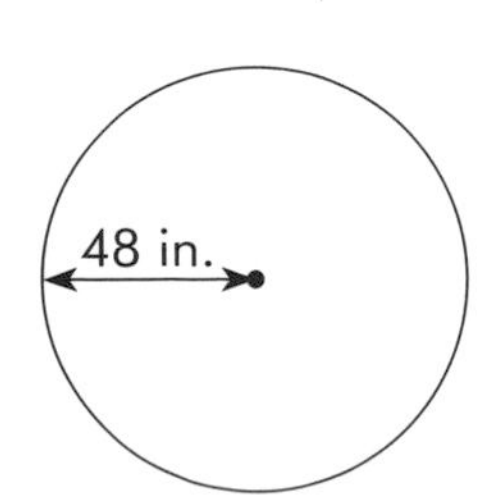

Radius = _____ in.

Circumference =

11. Find the perimeter of the figure shown below. (Use $\pi = \frac{22}{7}$)

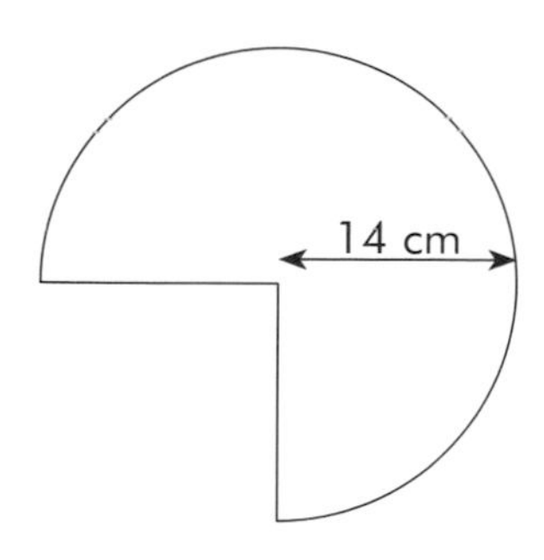

12. The figure below shows a semicircle enclosed in a rectangle. Find the perimeter of the shaded part. (Use $\pi = 3.14$)

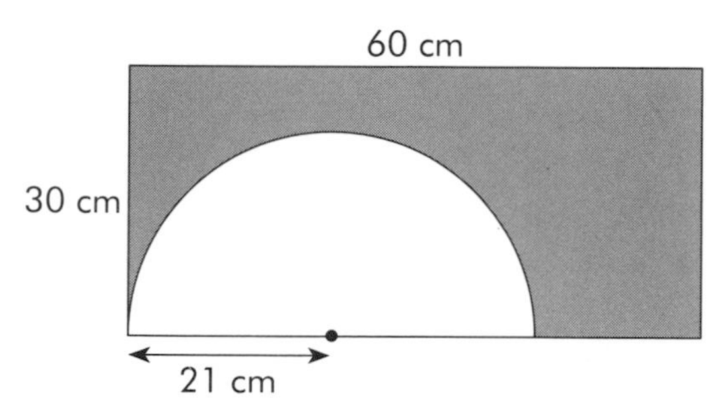

13. The figure below shows a semicircle and two identical quadrants enclosed in a rectangle. Find the perimeter of the shaded part. (Use $\pi = 3.14$)

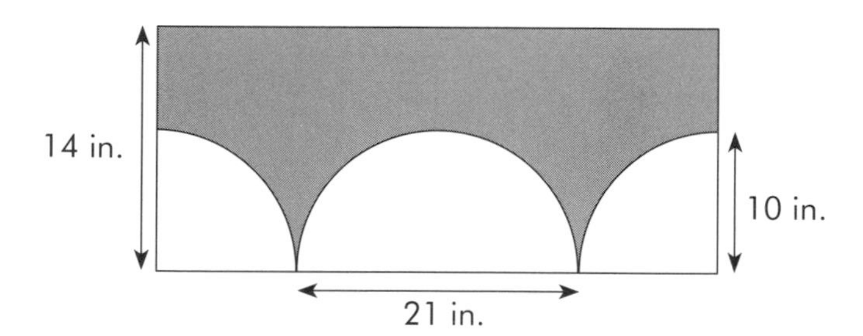

14. The figure below shows two identical semicircles enclosed in a square. Find the perimeter of the shaded part. (Use $\pi = \frac{22}{7}$)

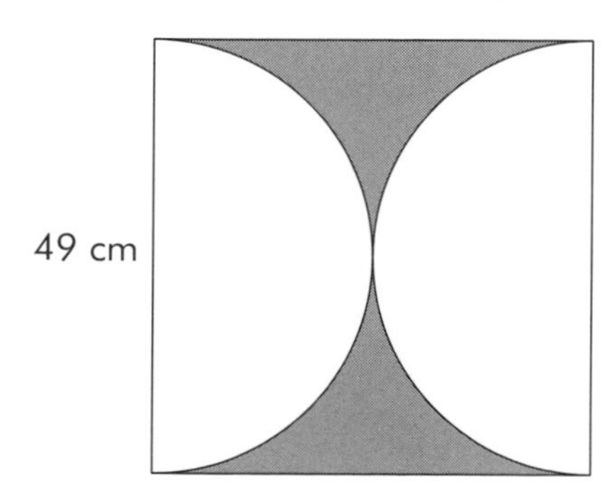

15. The figure below shows three identical semicircles and a square. Find the perimeter of the figure. (Use $\pi = 3.14$)

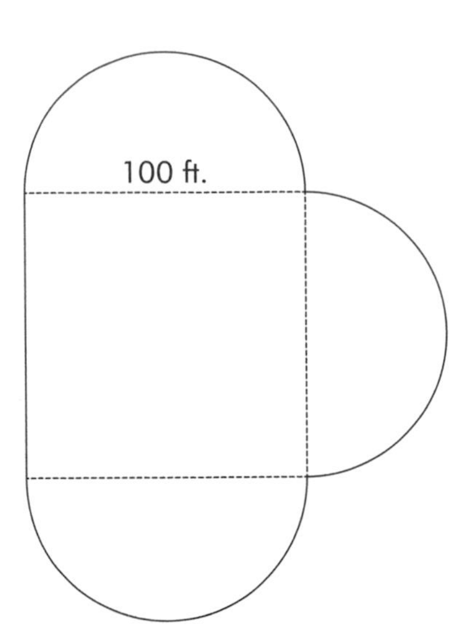

Calculate the area of each circle.

16.

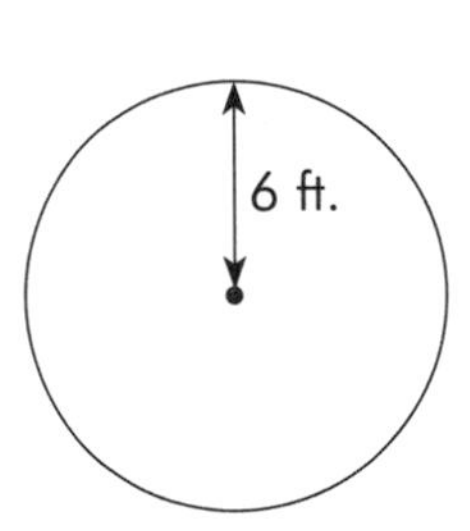

Area =

(Use $\pi = 3.14$)

17.

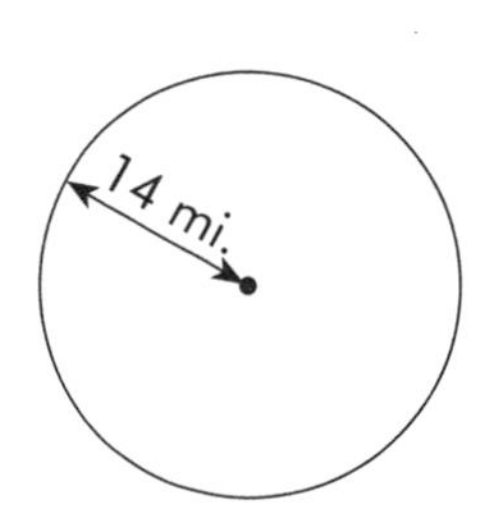

Area =

(Use $\pi = \frac{22}{7}$)

18.

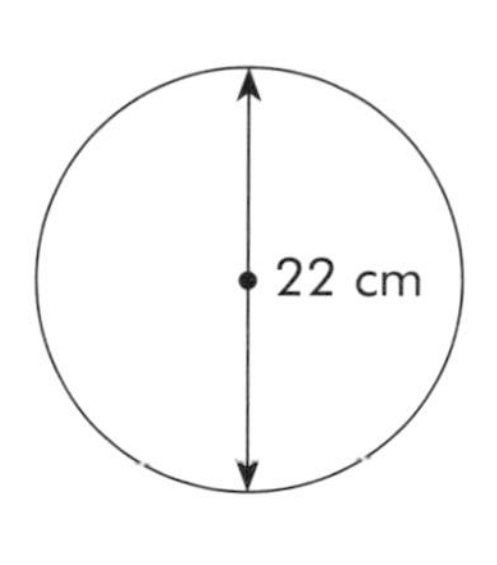

(Use $\pi = 3.14$)

Area =

19.

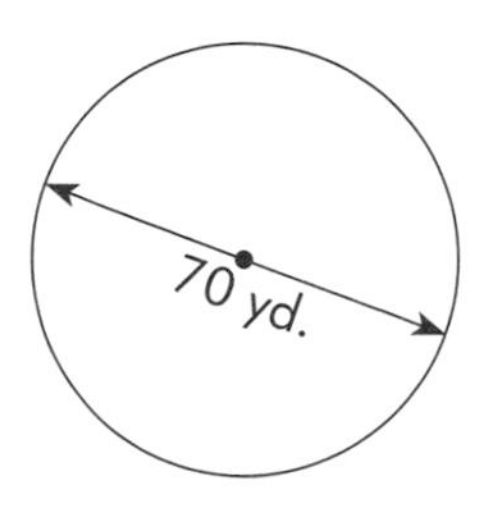

(Use $\pi = \frac{22}{7}$)

Area =

20.

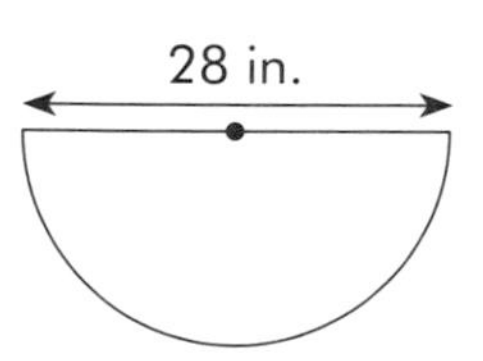

(Use $\pi = \frac{22}{7}$)

Area =

21.

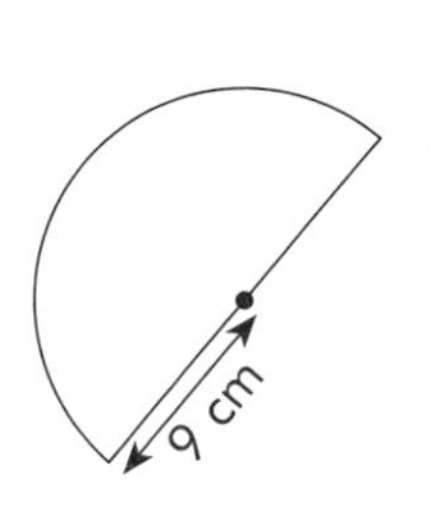

(Use $\pi = 3.14$)

Area =

22.

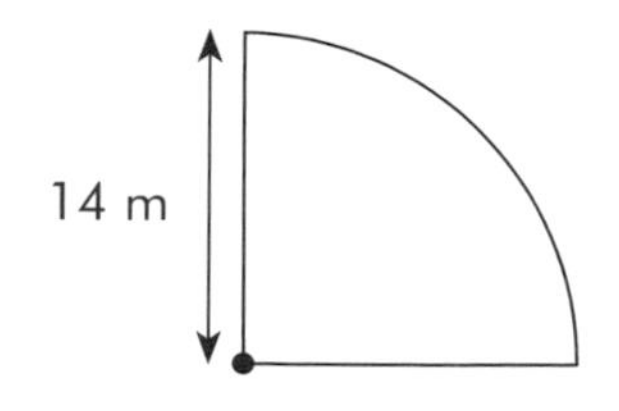

(Use $\pi = \frac{22}{7}$)

Area =

23.

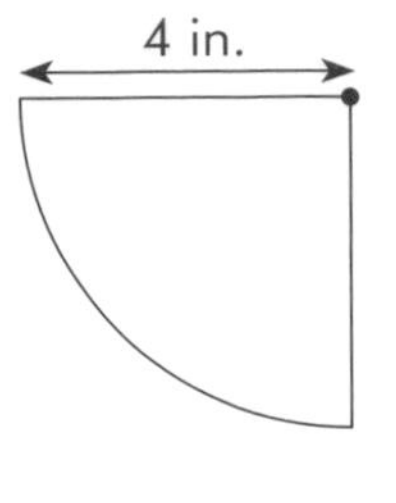

Area =

(Use $\pi = 3.14$)

24.

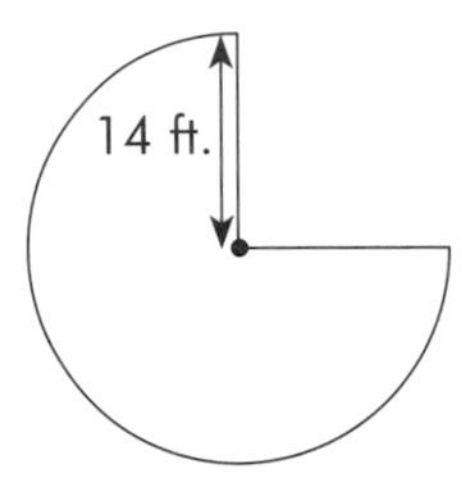

Area =

(Use $\pi = \frac{22}{7}$)

25.

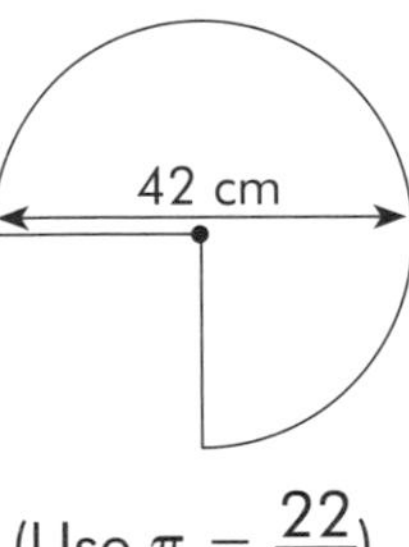

Area =

(Use $\pi = \frac{22}{7}$)

26. The figure below shows two identical semicircles enclosed in a circle. The diameter of the circle is 28 cm. The distance between the two semicircles is 8 cm. Find the area of the shaded part. (Use $\pi = 3.14$)

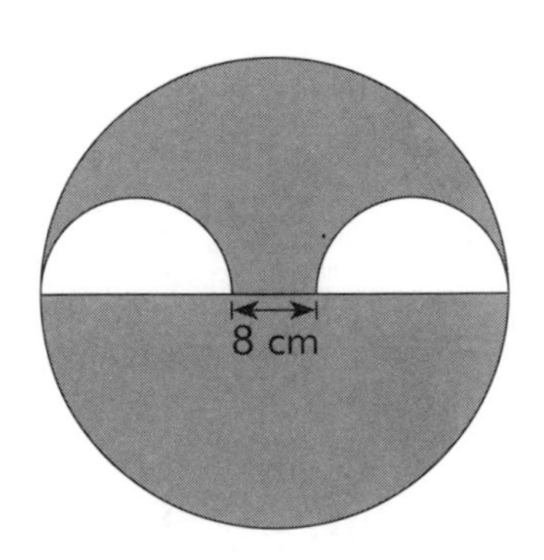

27. Two identical circles are enclosed in a square of side 70 in. Find the area of the shaded part. (Use $\pi = \frac{22}{7}$)

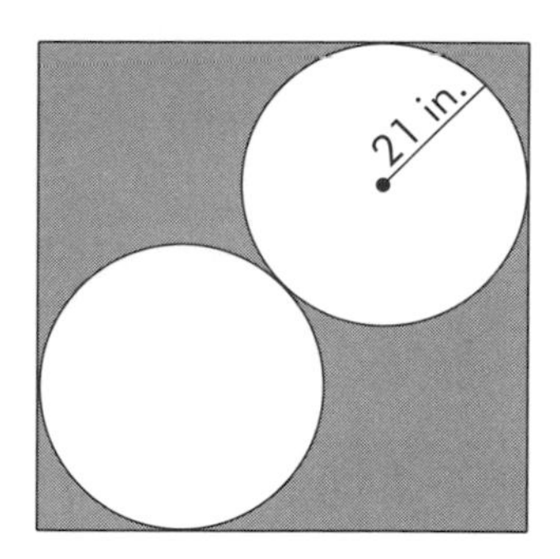

28. The figure below is made up of two circles. Find the area of the shaded part. (Use $\pi = 3.14$)

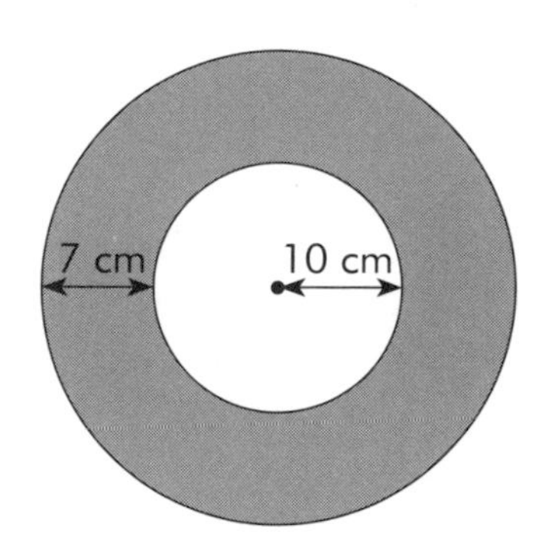

29. The figure below is made up of a semicircle and two identical quadrants. Find the area of the shaded part. (Use $\pi = \frac{22}{7}$)

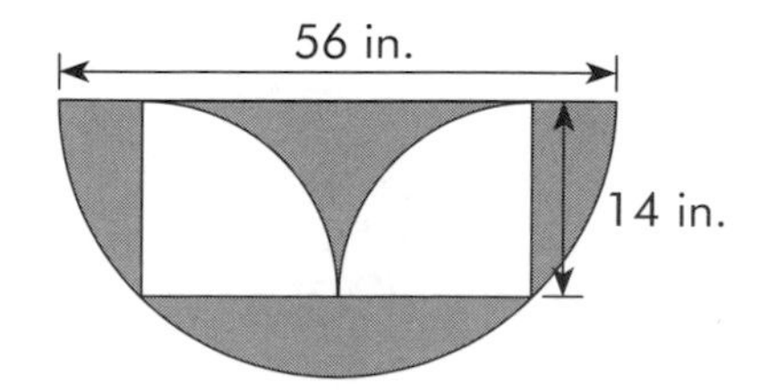

30. The figure below is made up of a circle and three identical small circles. The diameter of the bigger circle is 35 cm and the radius of each small circle is 7 cm. Find the area of the shaded part. (Use $\pi = 3.14$)

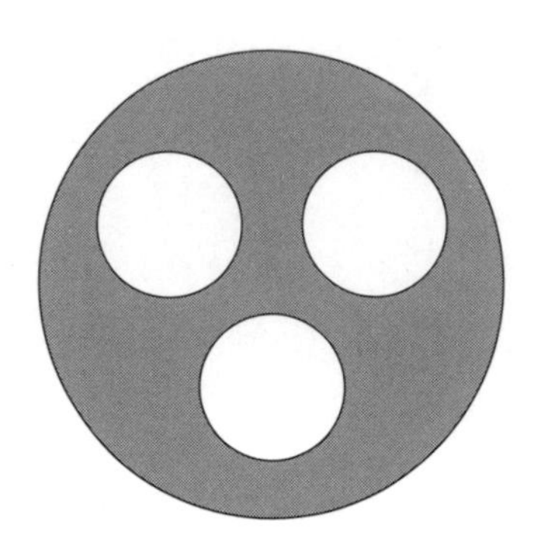

Write your answers on the lines.

31. Find the circumference of a frisbee with a radius of 10 in. (Use $\pi = 3.14$)

____

32. Mary bends a piece of wire into a semicircle as shown below. The diameter of the semicircle is 30 cm. What is the length of the piece of wire? (Use $\pi = 3.14$)

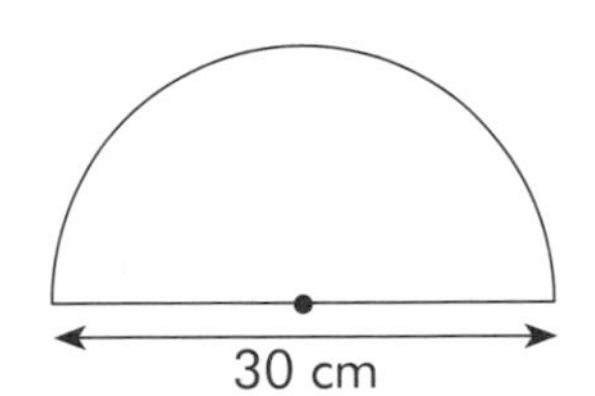

____

33. Find the circumference of a circle if its diameter is 21 ft. (Use $\pi = \frac{22}{7}$)

____

34. The diameter of a tire is 70 cm. How far does it travel when it makes 4 complete turns? (Use $\pi = \frac{22}{7}$)

____

35. A circular piece of cloth with a diameter of 60 in. is cut into four equal pieces through the center. What is the area of each piece of cloth? (Use $\pi = 3.14$)

36. Find the area of a quadrant with a radius of 63 cm. (Use $\pi = \frac{22}{7}$)

37. Find the area of the shaded part in the figure shown below. (Use $\pi = \frac{22}{7}$)

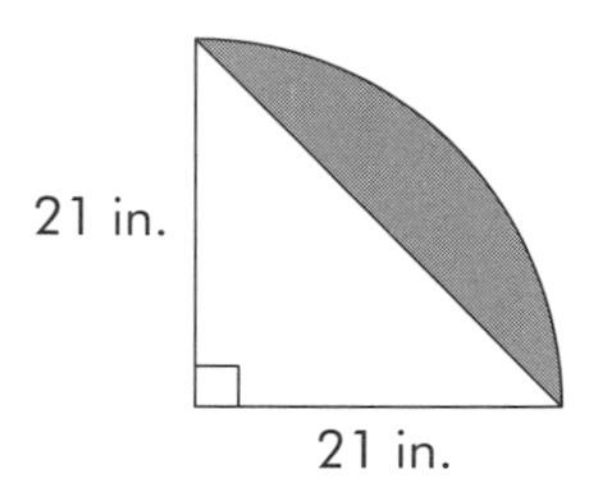

38. Find the area of a circle with a diameter of 34 cm. Write your answer in terms of π.

39. The figure below shows a square and two identical semicircles. What is the area of the shaded part? (Use $\pi = 3.14$)

22 ft.

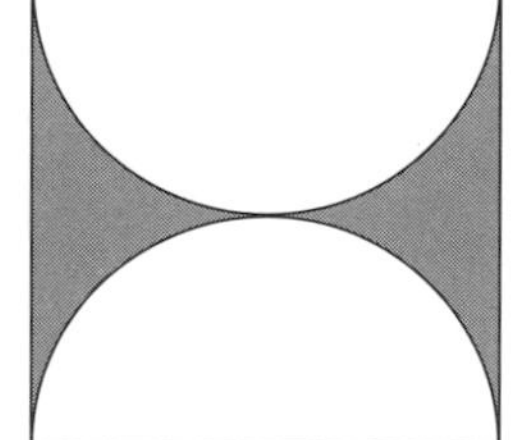

Solve the following story problems. Show your work in the space below.

40. The figure below shows a field that is made up of a rectangle and two identical semicircles. (Use $\pi = \frac{22}{7}$)

    (a) What is the area of the field?

    (b) If Anna runs around the field 8 times, how far does she run?

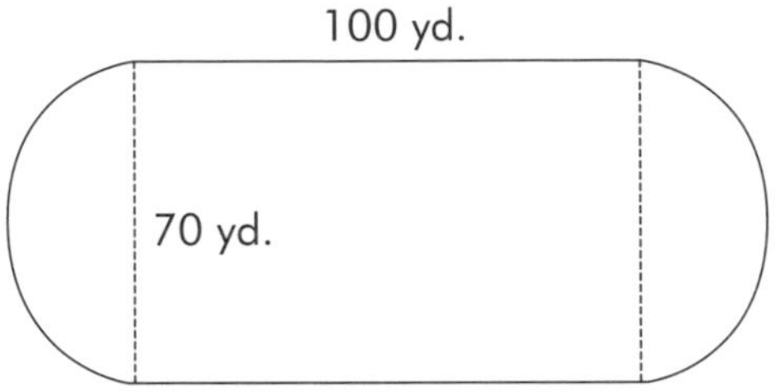

100 yd.

70 yd.

41. The figure below is made up of two identical large semicircles and three identical small semicircles. O is the center of the large semicircle. Find the length of the piece of wire needed to form this figure. (Use $\pi = 3.14$)

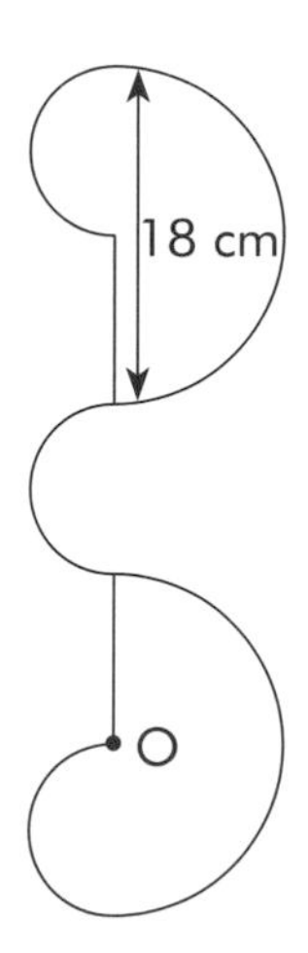

42. The figure below shows eight identical quadrants enclosed in a square. Every 2 quadrants overlap each other, forming a shaded portion. Find the area of the shaded portion in the figure. (Use $\pi = \frac{22}{7}$)

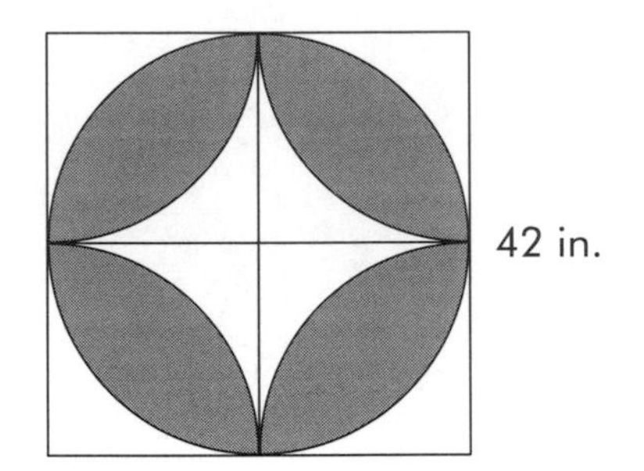

43. Four identical quadrants are placed inside a square of side 60 cm. Find the perimeter of the shaded part. (Use $\pi = 3.14$)

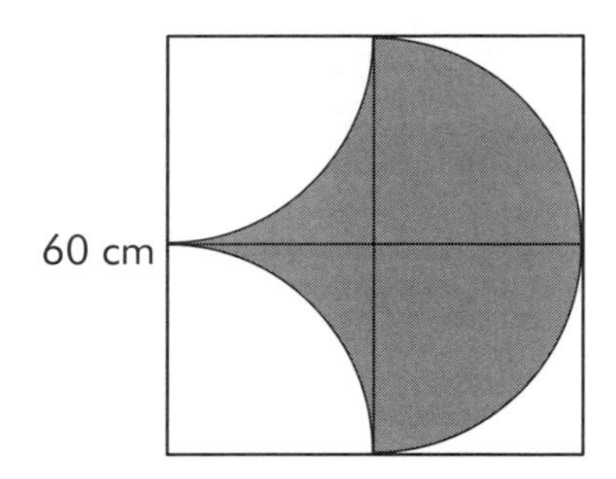

44. The figure below is made of a triangle and two semicircles. The sides of the triangle is 12 ft., 16 ft., and 20 ft. respectively. Find the area of the figure. (Use $\pi = \frac{22}{7}$)

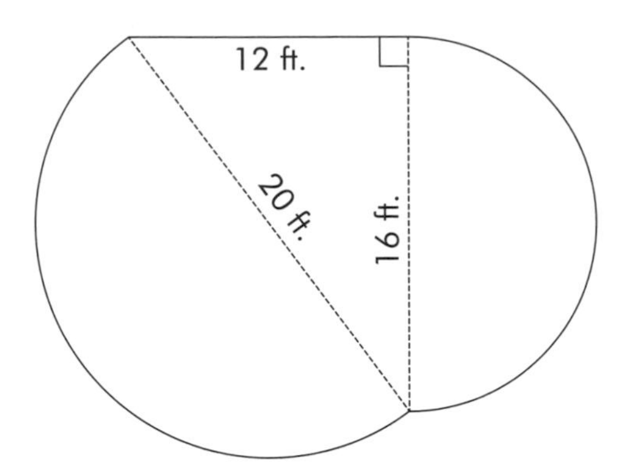

REVIEW 1

Choose the correct answer, and write its number in the parentheses. You may use a calculator whenever you see .

1. When Aqila rides her bicycle to her school at a rate of speed of 18 km/h, she takes 10 minutes to reach her school. If she decides to walk at a rate of speed of 4 km/h, how long will she take to reach her school?

   (1) 3 minutes (3) 15 minutes

   (2) 4.5 minutes (4) 45 minutes ( )

2. Statue A and Statue B are 865 ft. apart. Statue B and Statue C are 719 ft. apart. Find Ivan's average rate of speed when he walks from Statue C to Statue B in 18 minutes and from Statue B to Statue A in 30 minutes.

   (1) 23 ft. per min. (3) 33 ft. per min.

   (2) 28 ft. per min. (4) 39 ft. per min. ( )

3. The distance from Town A to Town B was 160 mi. Jaron left Town A at 6:00 A.M. and reached Town B at 2:00 A.M. the next day. How fast did he travel?

   (1) 10 mph (miles per hour) (3) 32 mph

   (2) 20 mph (4) 40 mph ( )

4. The radius of a circle is 8 cm. Its circumference is ________.

   (1) 4π cm (3) 16π cm

   (2) 8π cm (4) 64π cm ( )

5. The figure below shows a field. Mathew ran around the field twice. Find the total distance he ran. (Use $\pi = 3.14$)

   (1) 471 yd.

   (2) 621 yd.

   (3) 771 yd.

   (4) 1,542 yd. ( )

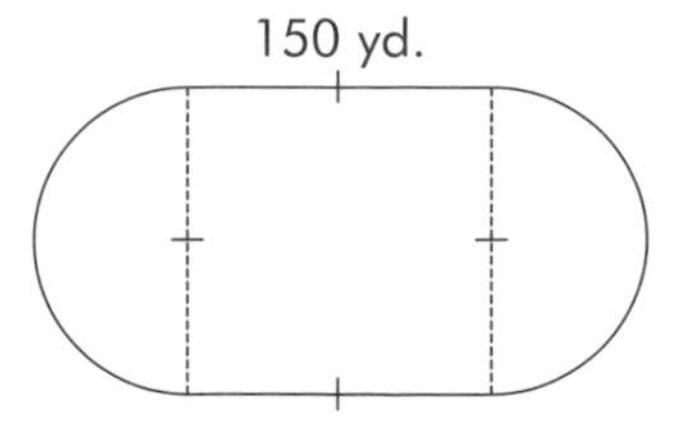

6. Mr. Carretero took $1\frac{1}{2}$ hours to travel a distance of 21 mi. He took another 2 hours to travel back the same route. What was his average rate of speed?

(1) 10.5 mph (3) 14 mph

(2) 12 mph (4) 21 mph ( )

7. The diameter of a circle is 12 cm. Find the circumference of the figure when two quadrants of the circle are removed. (Use $\pi = 3.14$)

(1) 18.84 cm

(2) 37.68 cm

(3) 42.84 cm

(4) 61.68 cm

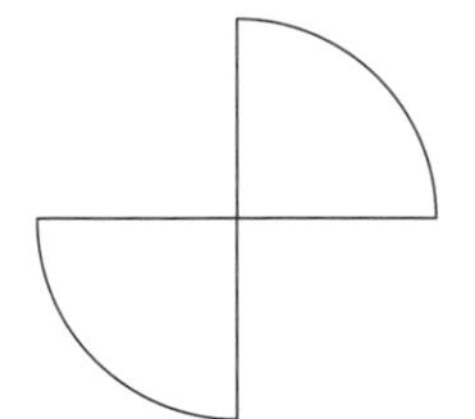

( )

Write your answers on the lines.

8. The figure below shows three semicircles. The diameter of the large circle is 70 in. Find the area of the figure. Write your answer in terms of π.

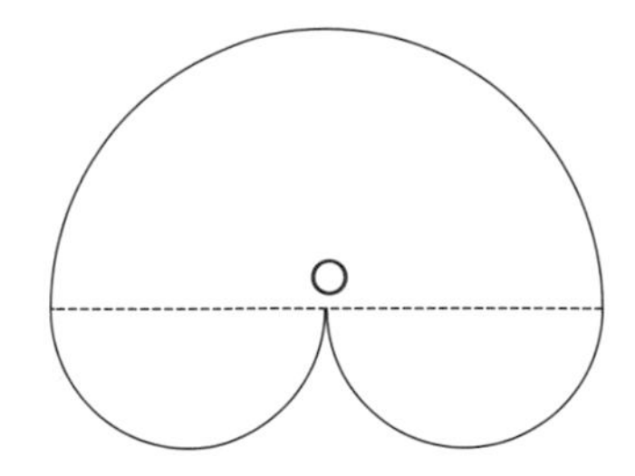

____

9. Cassandra can complete 60% of a 8-km route in 30 minutes. If she runs at a constant rate of speed, how long will she take to complete the whole route? Write your answer in minutes.

____

10. Michael drove at a rate of speed of 45 mph from his house to his office. It took him 42 minutes. If he were to decrease his rate of speed by 16%, how long would he need to travel from his office back home?

____

11. The figure below is made up of a quadrant and a semicircle. Find the perimeter of the shaded figure. (Use $\pi = \frac{22}{7}$)

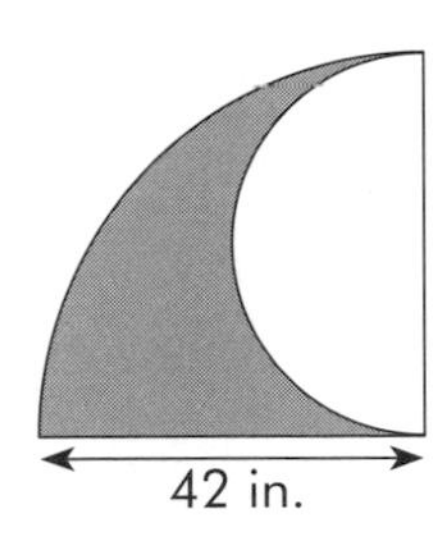

12. The figure below is made up of a square and a quadrant. The area of the square is 144 cm^2. Find the area of the shaded part. (Use $\pi = 3.14$)

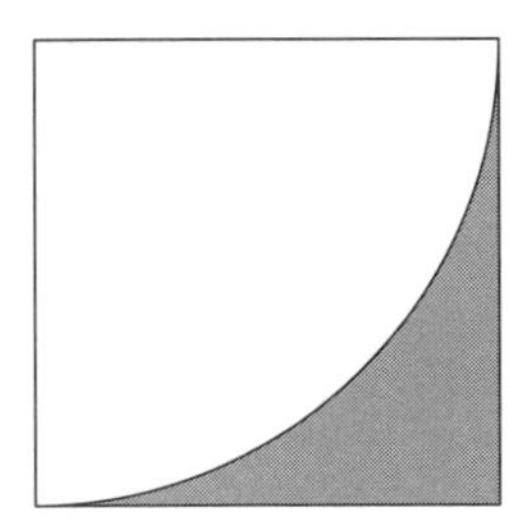

13. The figure below is made up of a small semicircle enclosed in a big semicircle. Find the area of the shaded part. (Use $\pi = \frac{22}{7}$)

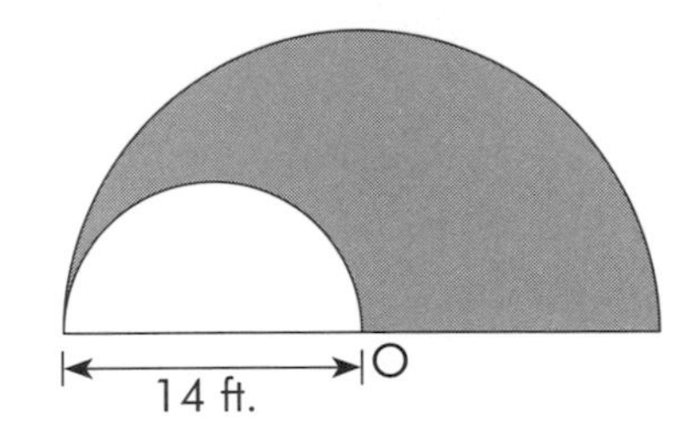

14. Mrs. Lenbury traveled 105 km at a rate of speed of 50 km/h. She still had to cover the remaining $\frac{1}{4}$ of the journey at a rate of speed of 25 km/h. How long did she take to cover the whole journey? Write your answer in hours.

15. The figure below is made up of an equilateral triangle and a quadrant. Find the perimeter of the figure. (Use $\pi = 3.14$)

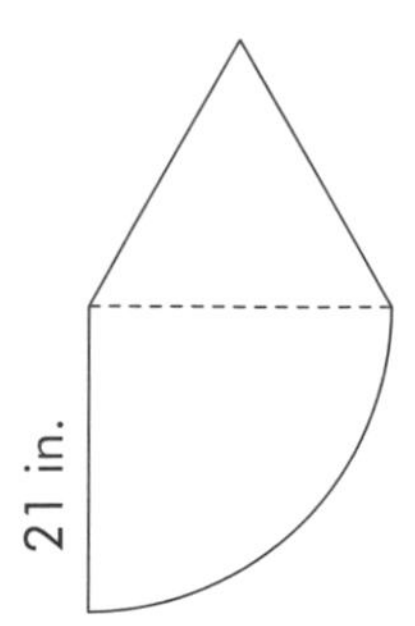

____

Solve the following story problems. Show your work in the space below.

16. Peter drives at a rate of speed of 28 mph to the beach. Anna drives at a rate of speed of 35 mph to the same destination. If Peter takes 15 minutes to drive from his house to the beach, how long will Anna take to drive the same distance?

17. A semicircle and a quadrant are enclosed in a rectangle as shown below. Find the area of the shaded part. (Use $\pi = 3.14$)

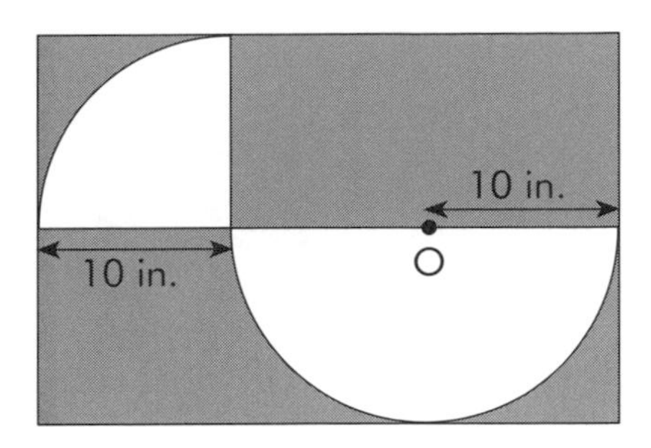

18. The figure below shows two identical circles and a rectangle. The radius of each circle is 28 in. Find the area of the shaded part. (Use $\pi = \frac{22}{7}$)

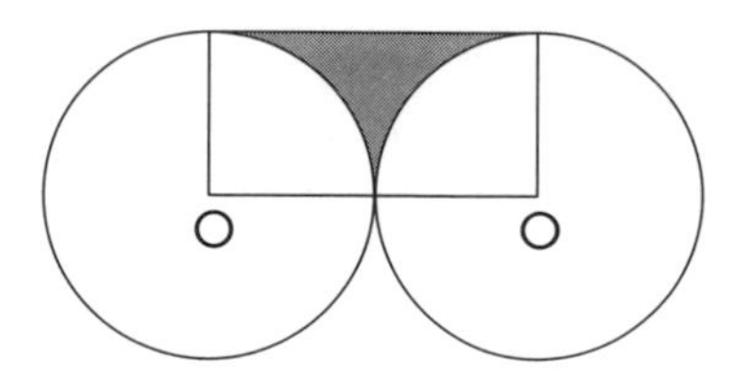

19. The figure below shows a semicircle and three identical quadrants removed from a square. The length of the square is four times the diameter of the semicircle. (Use $\pi = 3.14$)

(a) Find the area of the shaded part. Round your answer to the nearest whole number.

(b) Find the perimeter of the shaded part. Round your answer to the nearest whole number.

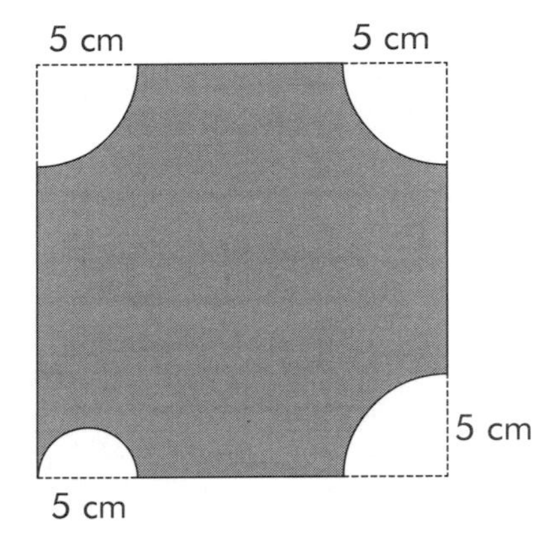

20. Travis left his house at 10:00 A.M. and traveled at an average rate of speed of 80 km/h. 2 hours later, Vanessa left the same house. She traveled the same route at a constant rate of speed. After Travis had traveled for 360 km, Vanessa caught up with him.

    (a) What was Vanessa's rate of speed?

    (b) How far apart would they be at 3:30 P.M.?

UNIT 9: PIE CHARTS

Examples:

The pie chart shows the different types of books read by Lilla in a month.

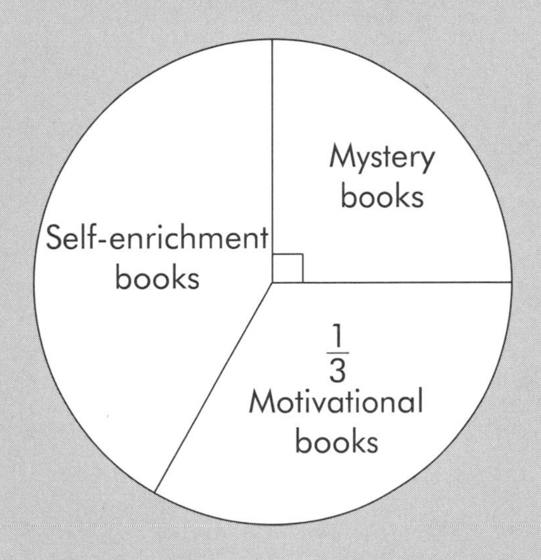

1. What fraction of the books read by Lilla was mystery? $\underline{\frac{1}{4}}$

2. If Lilla read 12 motivational books in that month, how many books did she read in all?

   $\frac{1}{3} \rightarrow 12$

   $\frac{3}{3} \rightarrow 3 \times 12 = 36$ <u>36 books</u>

3. How many self-enrichment books did Lilla read in that month?

   $\frac{1}{4} \times 36 = 9$ mystery books

   $36 - 12 - 9 = 15$

   <u>15 self-enrichment books</u>

Study each pie chart carefully. Write your answers on the lines. You may use a calculator whenever you see [calculator icon].

1. The pie chart below shows the number of students learning foreign languages at a school. Study it carefully, and answer the following questions.

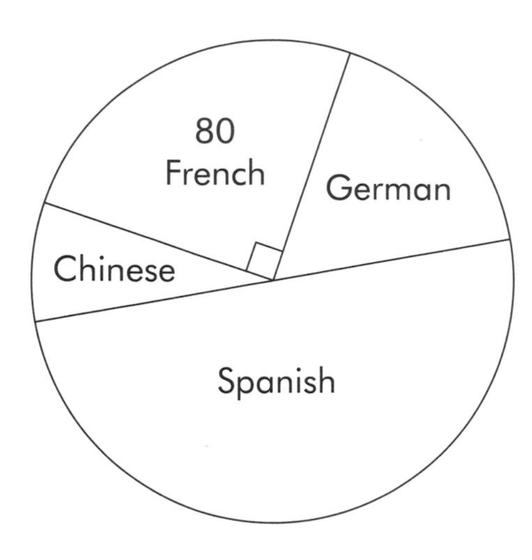

(a) The number of students learning Spanish is twice the number of those learning French. How many students are learning Spanish?

____

(b) How many students are learning a foreign language at the school?

____

(c) The number of students learning Chinese is $\frac{3}{20}$ of all students. How many students are learning Chinese?

____

(d) What fraction of the students are learning Spanish? ______________

2. The pie chart below represents the number of tourists staying at the Drexel Hotel in the month of November. Study it carefully and answer the following questions.

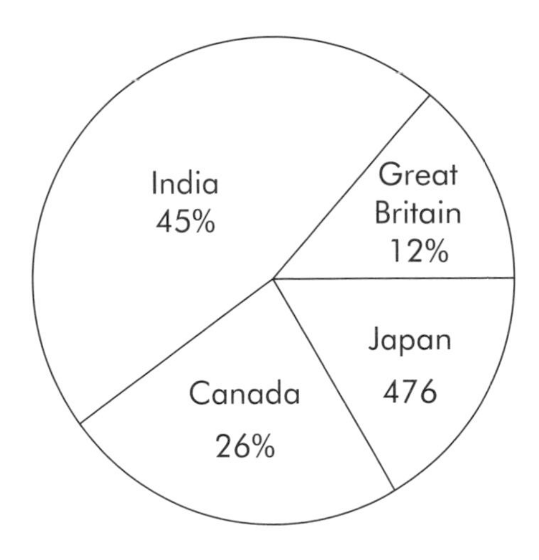

(a) What percentage of the tourists were from Japan?

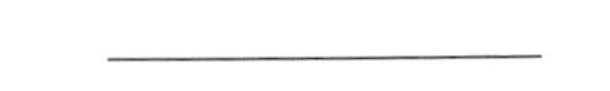

(b) What was the total number of tourists staying at the Drexel Hotel during November?

(c) How many more Canadian tourists than British tourists stayed at the Drexel Hotel during November?

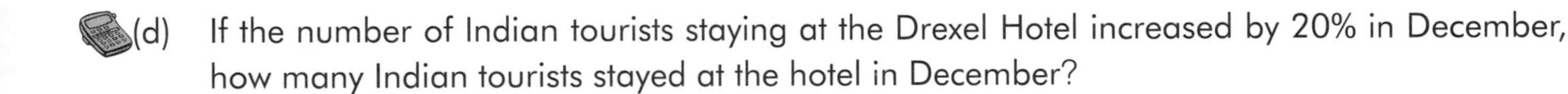

(d) If the number of Indian tourists staying at the Drexel Hotel increased by 20% in December, how many Indian tourists stayed at the hotel in December?

3. The pie chart below represents 360 families living in a neighborhood. Study it carefully, and answer the following questions.

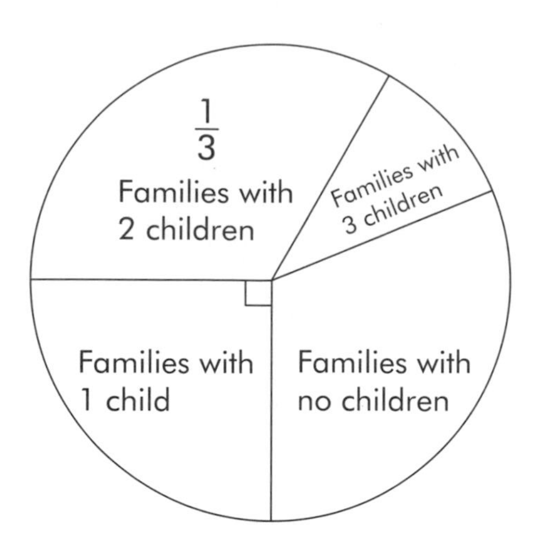

(a) How many families have 2 children?

____

(b) Find the total number of families with 3 children and with no children.

____

(c) The ratio of families with no children to families with 3 children is 4:1. How many families have no children?

____

(d) Find the total number of children in the neighborhood.

____

4. The pie chart below represents the different hobbies of a group of students who took part in a survey. Study it carefully, and answer the following questions.

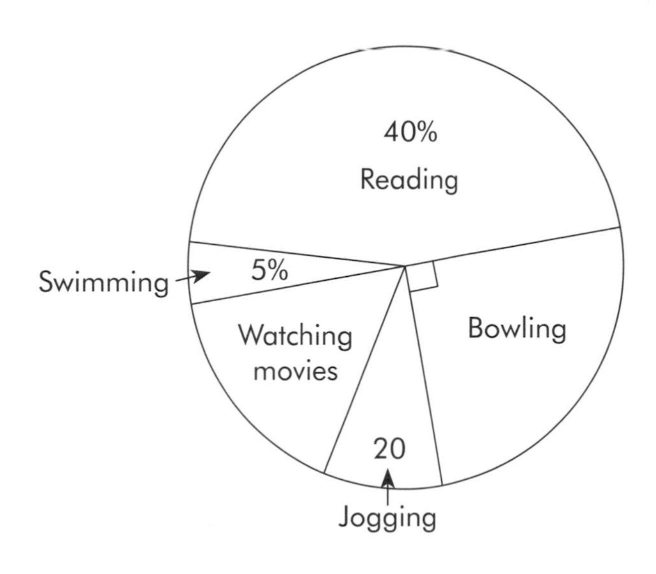

(a) If the number of students who liked jogging is $\frac{2}{5}$ the number of students who liked bowling, how many students took part in the survey?

____

(b) What percentage of the students liked to watch movies and jogging?

____

(c) What was the difference between the number of students who liked to read and those who liked to swim?

____

(d) 10% of the girls who took part in the survey liked swimming. If half of those who liked swimming were girls, how many girls took part in the survey?

____

5. The pie chart below represents the number of ice-cream cones sold at a shop. Study it carefully, and answer the following questions.

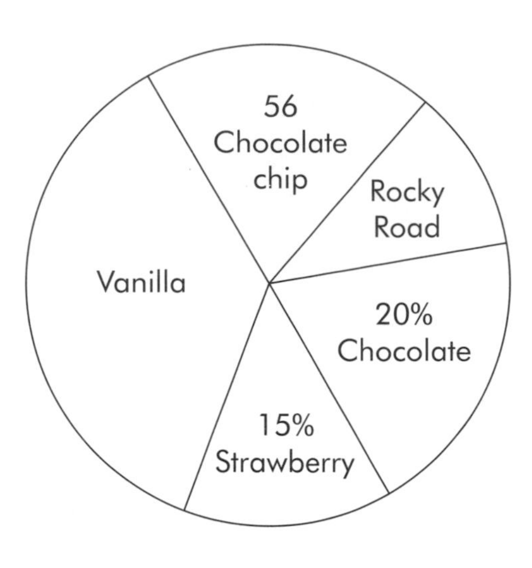

(a) The ratio of Rocky Road ice-cream cones to chocolate chip ice-cream cones to vanilla ice-cream cones sold at the shop was 2:4:7. How many Rocky Road and vanilla ice-cream cones were sold?

____

(b) How many strawberry and chocolate ice-cream cones were sold?

____

(c) The shop sold the same number of ____________ and ____________ ice-cream cones.

(d) How many ice-cream cones were sold in all? ______________

6. The pie chart below shows Leena's monthly budget after a pay raise. Study it carefully, and answer the following questions.

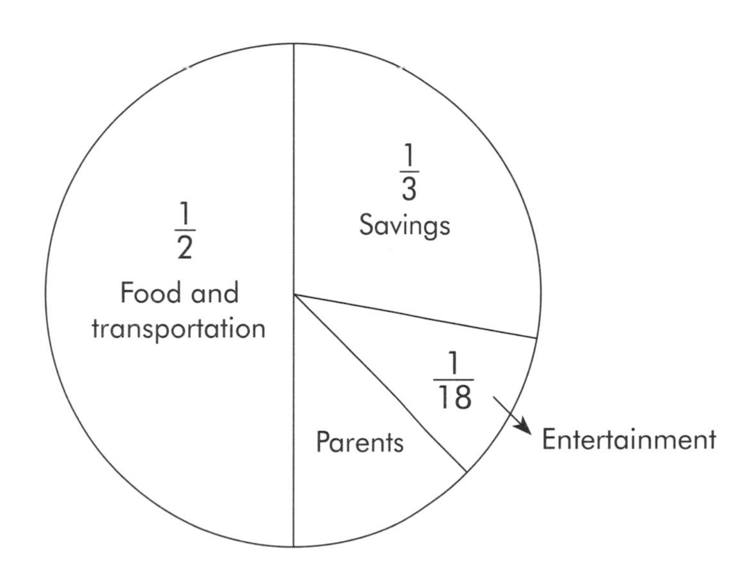

(a) If Leena spends $540 on food and 75% as much on transportation, how much does she spend on food and transportation?

____

(b) How much money does Leena give to her parents in a month?

____

(c) How much money does Leena save in a year? ____________

(d) If Leena's current salary is 20% more than before, find her monthly salary before the pay raise.

____

7. The pie chart below shows the different types of assessment books sold at a school bookstore. Line XY divides the pie chart into two equal parts. Study it carefully, and answer the following questions.

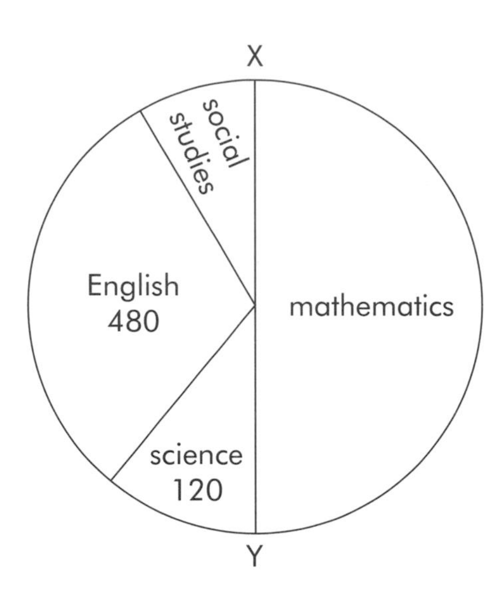

(a) The number of social studies assessment books sold was 20% of the number of mathematics assessment books sold. How many mathematics assessment books were sold in all?

____

(b) Find the difference between the number of social studies assessment books and the number of English assessment books sold at the school bookstore.

____

(c) What was the total number of science and mathematics assessment books sold at the school bookstore?

____

(d) What percentage of the total number of assessment books sold at the school bookstore were English assessment books?

____

8. The pie chart below shows the number of tourists who visited a few places of interest one Sunday. Study it carefully, and answer the following questions.

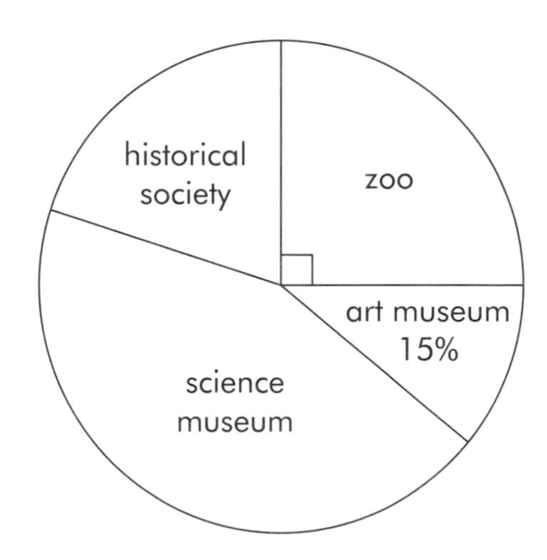

(a) The number of tourists who visited the historical society was $\frac{4}{5}$ the number of tourists who visited the zoo. If 420 tourists went to the historical society, how many tourists were there in all?

____

(b) How many more tourists went to the zoo than to the art museum?

____

(c) How many tourists went to the science museum?

____

(d) What percentage of the tourists went to the science museum?

____

9. The pie chart below shows the number of books in a library. Study it carefully, and answer the following questions.

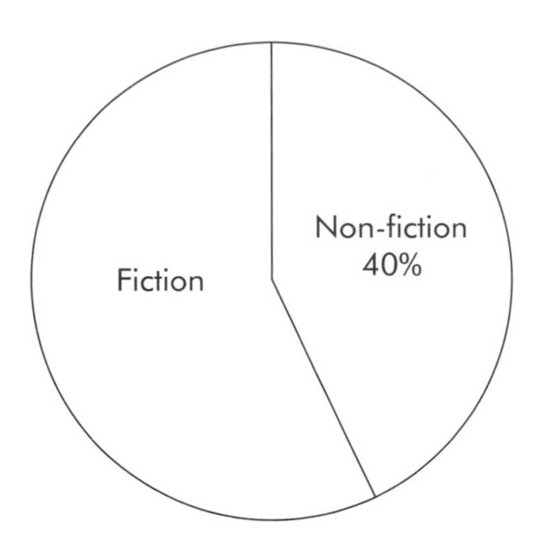

(a) $\frac{1}{5}$ of the fiction books are non-English. What percentage of the books in the library are non-English fiction?

____

(b) There are 2,700 more English fiction books than non-English fiction books. How many fiction books are there in the library?

____

(c) How many fiction and non-fiction books are there in the library?

____

(d) If 15% of the non-fiction books are non-English, what is the ratio of non-English non-fiction books to the total number of library books?

____

10. The pie chart below shows how an amount of money is shared among four sisters. Study it carefully, and answer the following questions.

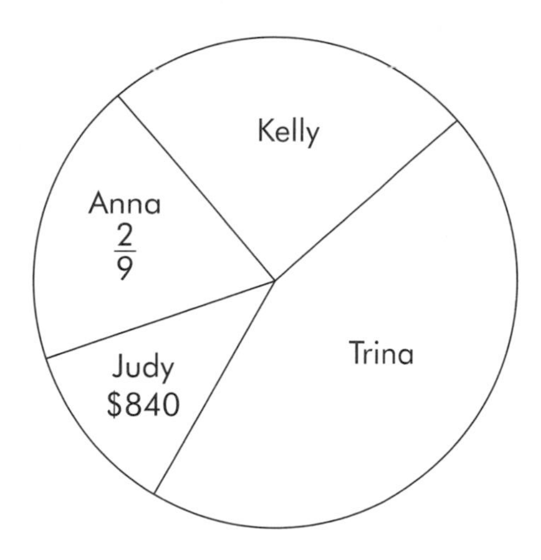

(a) The ratio of Judy's share to Trina's share is 7:12. How much does Trina get?

____

(b) If the sum of money is $4,320, how much is Anna's share?

____

(c) What is the difference between Kelly's share and Anna's share?

____

(d) What is the ratio of Anna's share to Trina's share to the total sum of money?

____

UNIT 10: AREA AND PERIMETER

Examples:

The figure below is made up of 2 identical right triangles and 2 identical triangles.

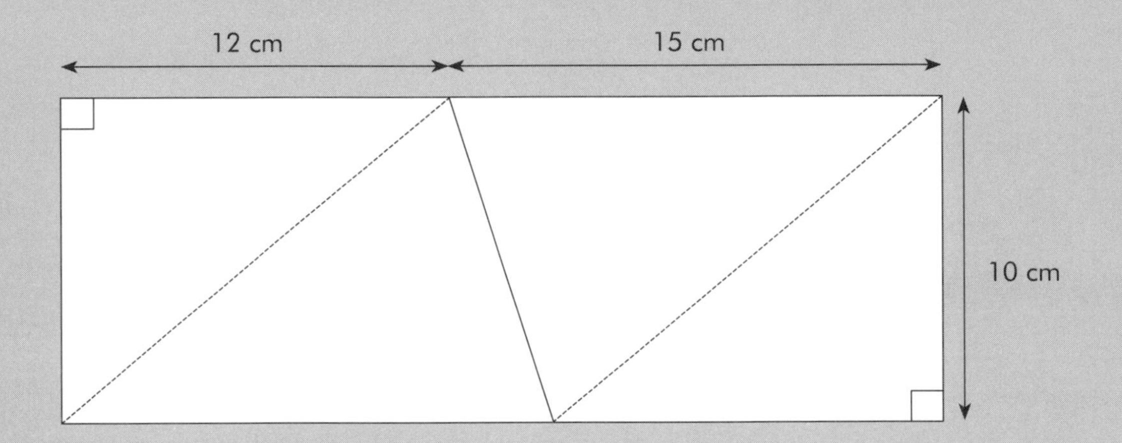

1. Find the area of the figure.

   Area of each right triangle $= \frac{1}{2} \times 12 \times 10 = 60$ cm²

   Area of each triangle $= \frac{1}{2} \times 15 \times 10 = 75$ cm²

   $60 + 75 + 75 + 60 = 270$ cm²

   The area of the figure is **270 cm²**.

2. Find the perimeter of the figure.

   $10 + 12 + 15 + 10 + 12 + 15 = 74$ cm

   The perimeter of the figure is **74 cm**.

Solve the following problems. Show your work in the space below.

1. The figure on the right is made up of 2 rectangles.

   (a) Find the area of the figure.

   (b) Find the perimeter of the figure.

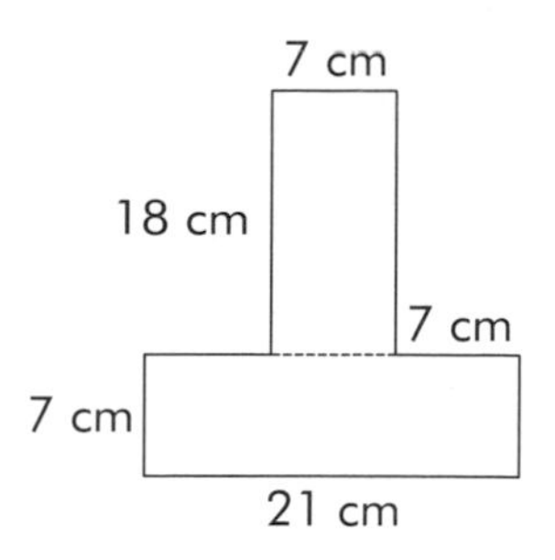

2. The figure below shows a semicircle in an equilateral triangle of side 28 in. The height of the triangle is 20 in. If the diameter of the semicircle is 14 in., find the area of the shaded part. (Use $\pi = \frac{22}{7}$)

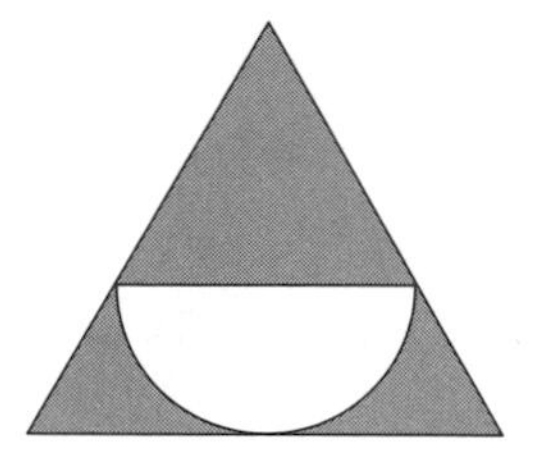

3. The figure below shows two identical isosceles triangles in a rectangle.

   (a) Find the area of the shaded part.

   (b) Find the perimeter of the shaded part.

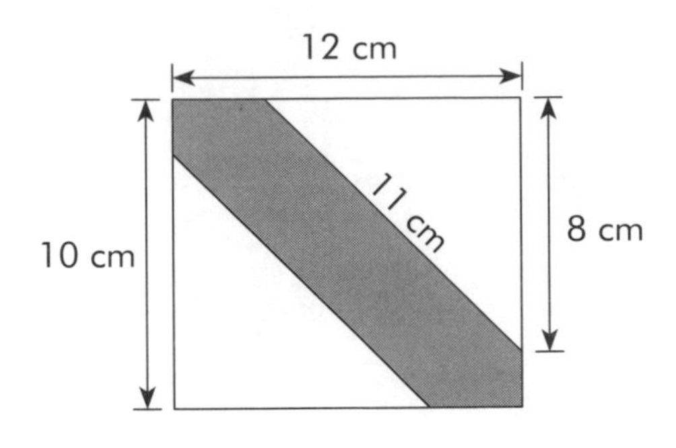

4. The figure below shows a quadrant in a square. Find the area of the shaded portion. (Use $\pi = \frac{22}{7}$)

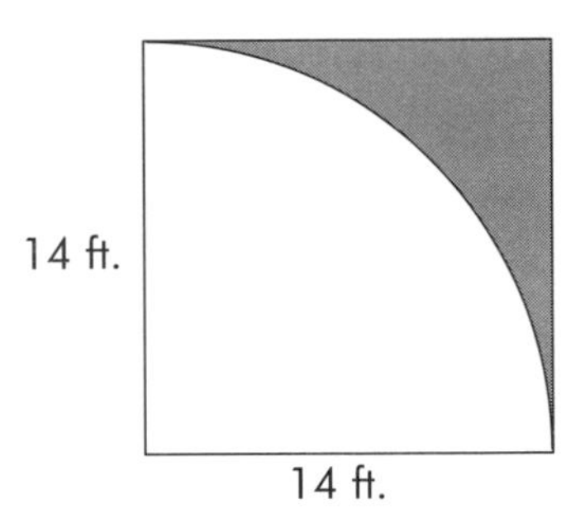

5. The figure below shows two identical triangles in a rectangle. Find the area of the shaded part.

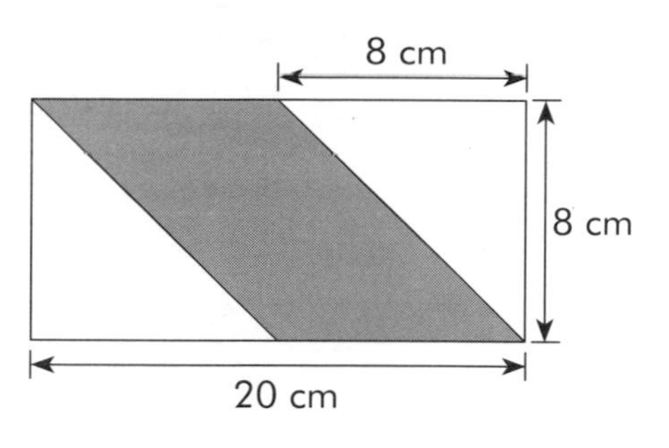

6. In the figure below, ABCD is a square. There are two triangles in square ABCD. Find the area of the shaded part.

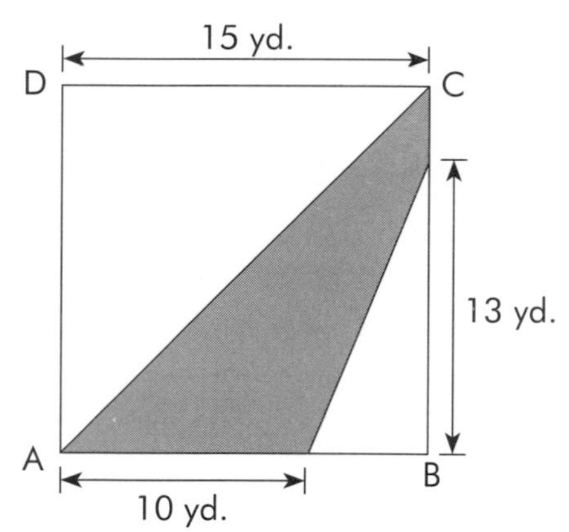

7. The figure below shows a trapezoid. Find its area.
(Hint: You can divide the trapezoid into a rectangle and a triangle.)

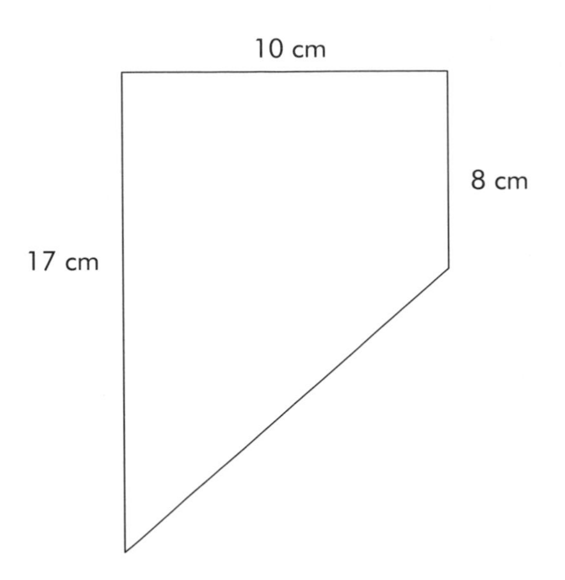

8. (a) Find the perimeter of the figure.

(b) Find the area of the figure.

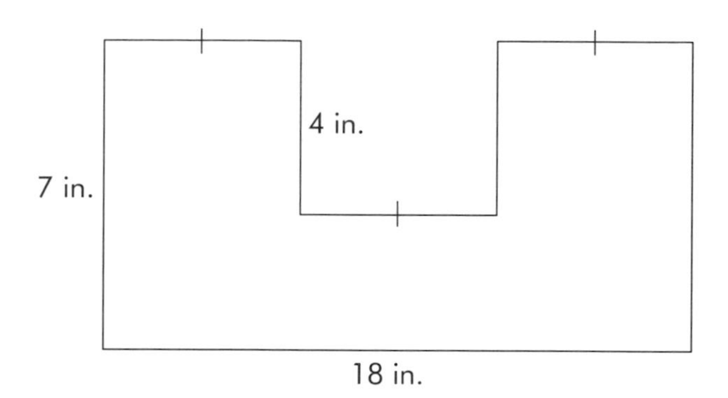

9. The figure below is made up of 8 identical triangles. Find the area of the shaded parts.

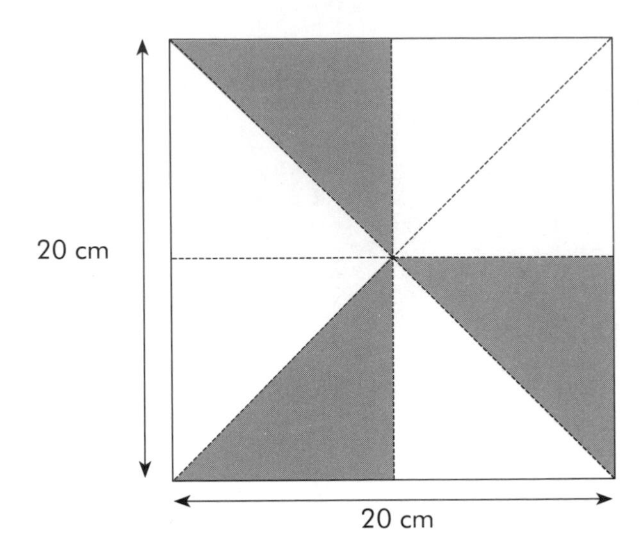

10. The figure below shows an egg tray. Find the area of the shaded portion. (Use $\pi = 3.14$)

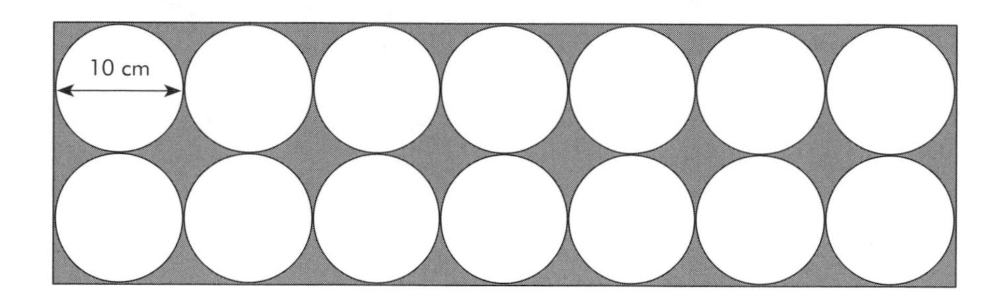

REVIEW 2

Choose the correct answer, and write its number in the parentheses. You may use a calculator whenever you see [calculator icon].

The pie chart below shows how Desmond spent $192 that his father gave him. Study it carefully, and answer questions 1 to 3.

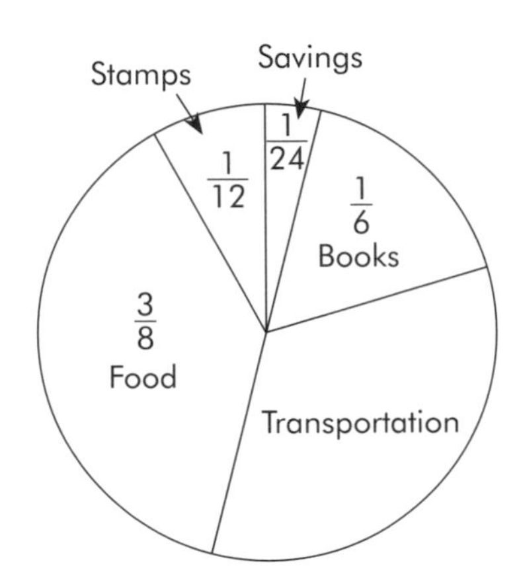

1. How much money did Desmond spend on books and stamps?

(1)	$16	(3)	$48	
(2)	$32	(4)	$80	( )

2. How much money did Desmond spend on food and transportation?

(1)	$56	(3)	$72	
(2)	$64	(4)	$136	( )

3. How much money did Desmond save?

(1)	$8	(3)	$24	
(2)	$16	(4)	$32	( )

4. The figure below shows a trapezoid and a triangle. Find the area of the figure.

(1) 60 cm^2
(2) 94 cm^2
(3) 110 cm^2
(4) 143 cm^2

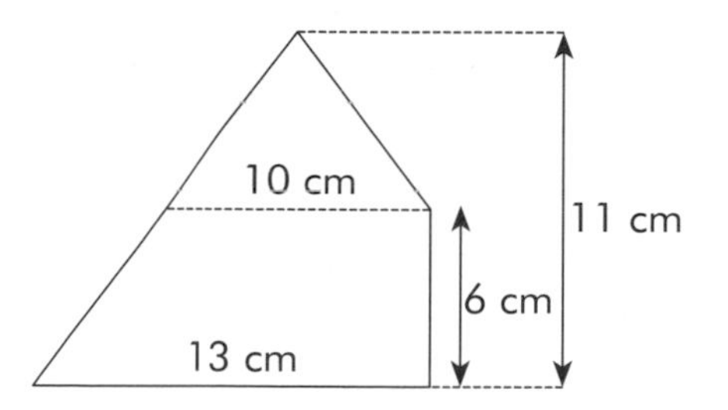

( )

5. The figure below is made up of two triangles. Find the area of the figure.

(1) 180 $in.^2$
(2) 216 $in.^2$
(3) 288 $in.^2$
(4) 360 $in.^2$

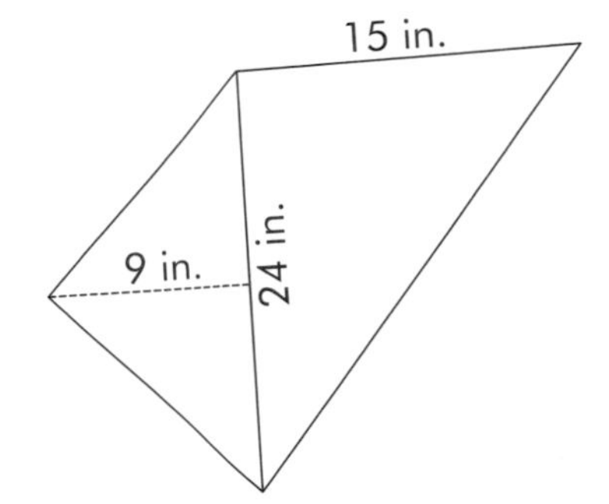

( )

6. The figure below is made up of a square and a semicircle. If each side of the square is 20 cm, find the perimeter of the figure. (Use $\pi = 3.14$)

(1) 31.4 cm
(2) 62.8 cm
(3) 91.4 cm
(4) 122.8 cm

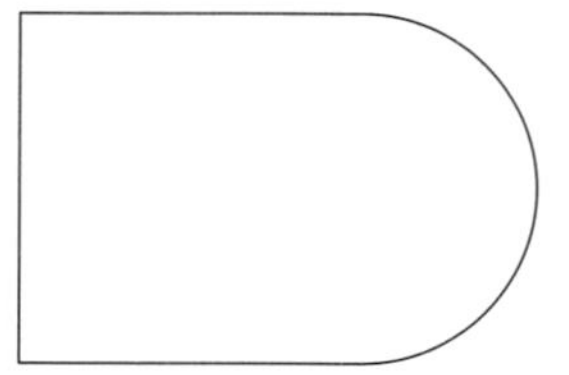

( )

7. The figure below shows a circle in a rectangle. Find the shaded area. (Use $\pi = \frac{22}{7}$)

(1) 1,386 cm^2
(2) 2,142 cm^2
(3) 3,528 cm^2
(4) 5,544 cm^2

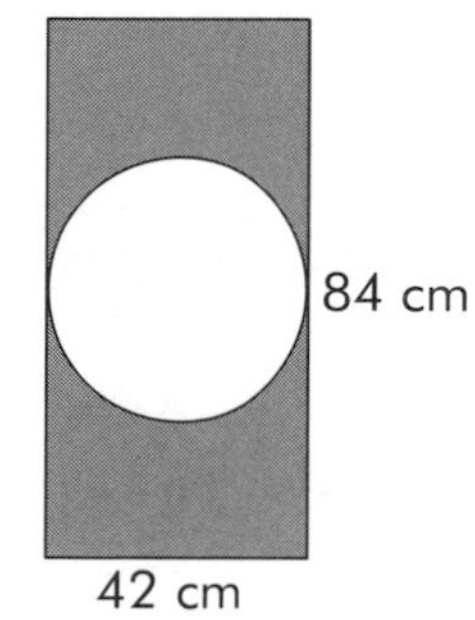

( )

Write your answers on the lines.

8. Mandy cut a circle with a radius of 14 in. from a piece of rectangular cardboard. Find the area of the remaining cardboard. (Use $\pi = \frac{22}{7}$)

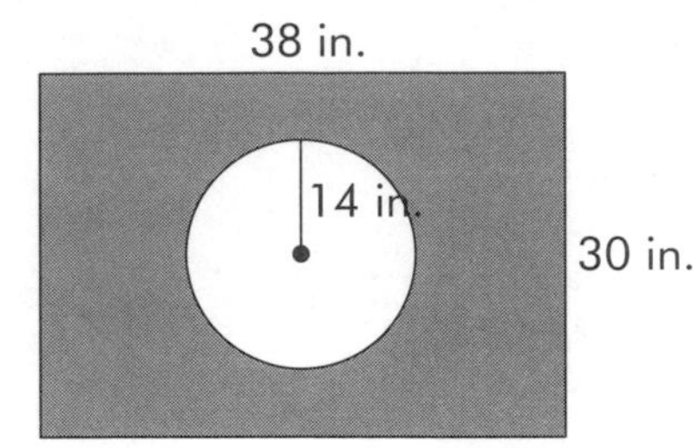

9. During an art lesson, Luca created a repeated pattern on a sheet of paper as shown below. Find the total area of the shaded parts.

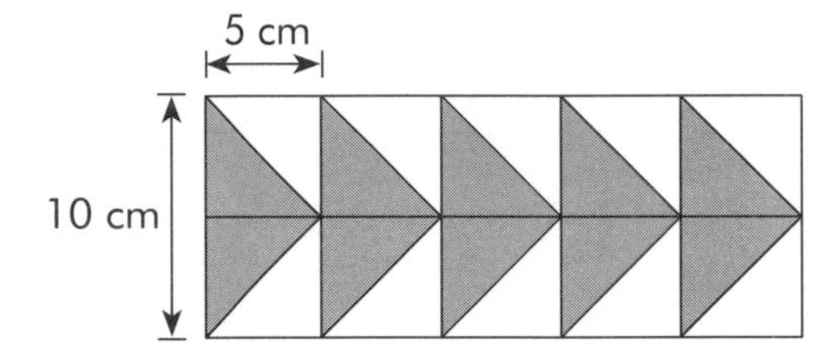

The pie chart below shows the different activities that a class of students enjoys doing during free time. Study it carefully, and answer questions 10 to 12.

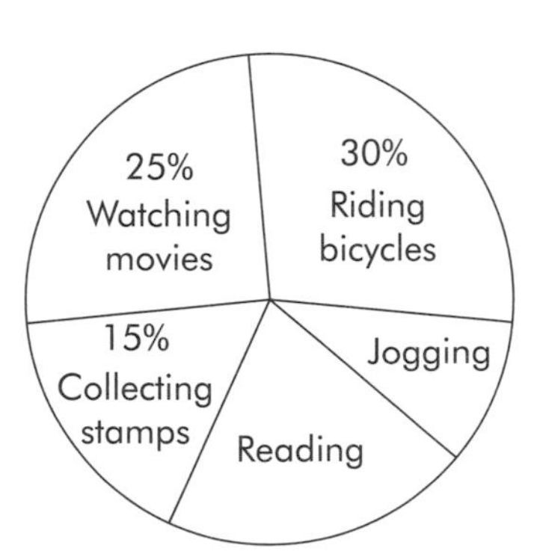

10. If 12 students like riding bicycles, how many students are in the class?

11. How many students like watching movies?

12. If the number of students who like reading is twice the number of students who like jogging, how many students like to read?

13. The figure below is made up of two rectangles and two identical squares. Find its perimeter.

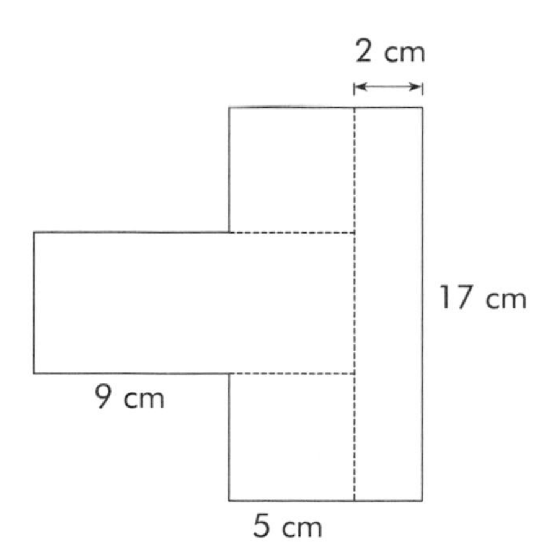

____

14. Find the area of the figure shown below.

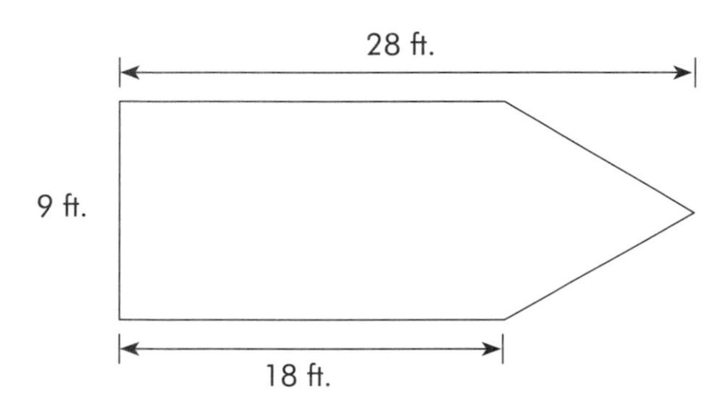

____

15. The figure below shows a baking tray. Find the area of the shaded part. (Use $\pi = 3.14$)

14 cm

5 cm

14 cm

____

Solve the following story problems. Show your work in the space below.

The pie chart below shows the amount of fruit sold by a cashier. Study it carefully, and answer questions 16 and 17 below.

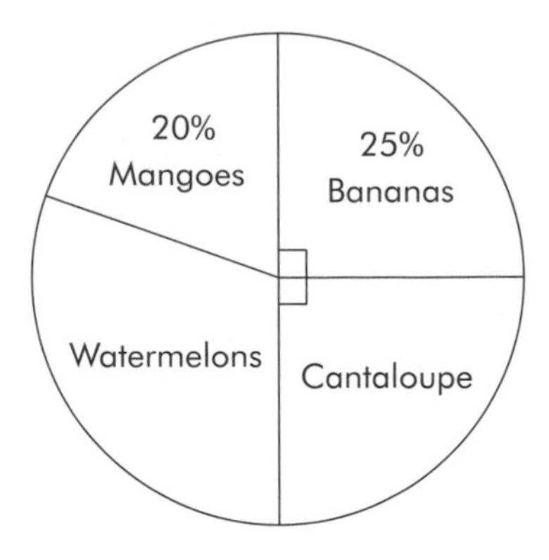

16. If the cashier sold 300 pieces of fruit altogether, how many watermelons did he sell?

17. How much money would he make from the sale of cantaloupes and mangoes if he sold each cantaloupe at $1.30 and each mango at $1.60?

18. A puzzle measures 120 cm by 60 cm. A piece, missing from the puzzle, is shown below. What is the area of the remaining puzzle? (Use $\pi = 3.14$)

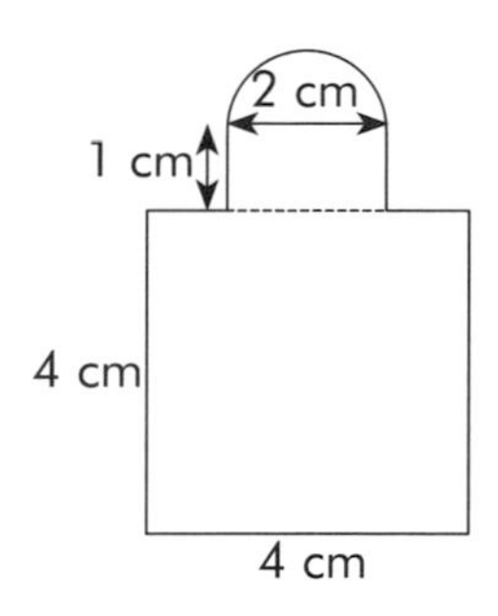

19. Mrs. Rung wants to make a display sign on her gate. Find the area of the display sign.

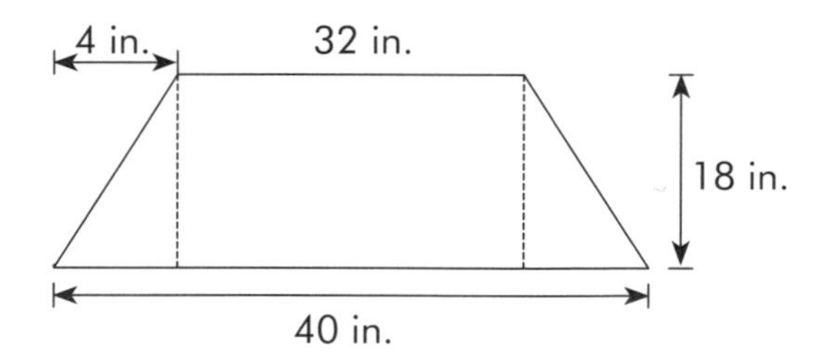

20. The figure is made up of a rectangle and 6 semicircles. Find the perimeter of the figure. (Use $\pi = \frac{22}{7}$)

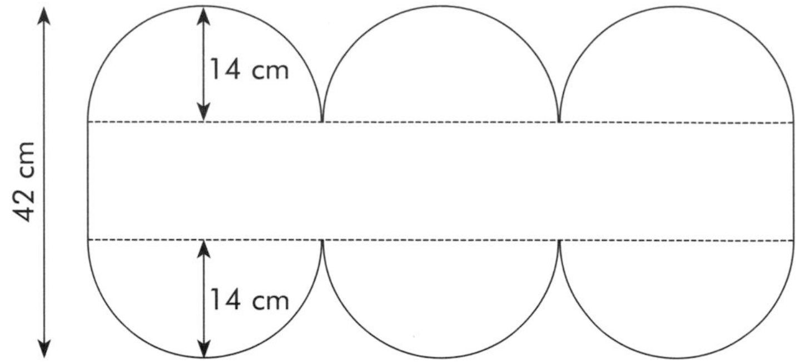

14 cm

42 cm

14 cm

Unit 11: VOLUME

Examples:

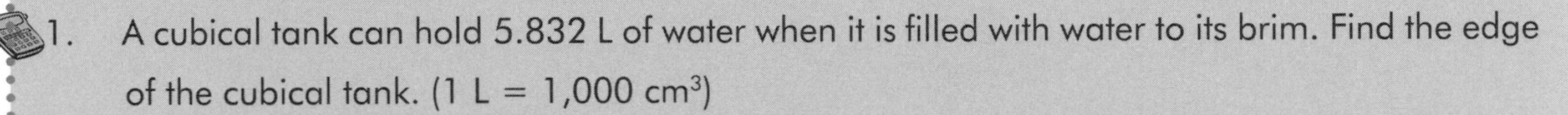

1. A cubical tank can hold 5.832 L of water when it is filled with water to its brim. Find the edge of the cubical tank. (1 L = 1,000 cm^3)

   $5.832 \times 1{,}000 = 5{,}832 \text{ cm}^3$

   $\sqrt[3]{5{,}832} = 18 \text{ cm}$

   The edge of the cubical tank is **18 cm**.

2. A rectangular tank is $\frac{1}{4}$ filled with water. The volume of water in the tank is 3,500 cubic inches (in.^{3}). The base area of the tank is 700 in.^{2} Find the height of the tank.

   $\frac{1}{4} \rightarrow 3{,}500 \text{ in.}^3$

   $4 \times 3{,}500 = 14{,}000 \text{ in.}^3$

   $14{,}000 \div 700 = 20 \text{ in.}$

   The height of the tank is **2 in.**

Use a calculator to find the square root of the following.

1. $\sqrt{529} =$

2. $\sqrt{1{,}225} =$

3. $\sqrt{324} =$

4. $\sqrt{1{,}936} =$

5. $\sqrt{2{,}304} =$

Use a calculator to find the cube root of the following.

6. $\sqrt[3]{512}$ =

7. $\sqrt[3]{729}$ =

8. $\sqrt[3]{1,728}$ =

9. $\sqrt[3]{6,859}$ =

10. $\sqrt[3]{2,744}$ =

Find the volume of each solid.

11.

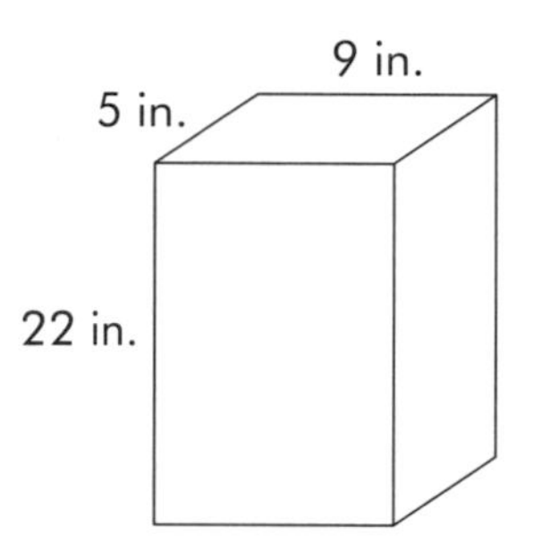

Volume =

12.

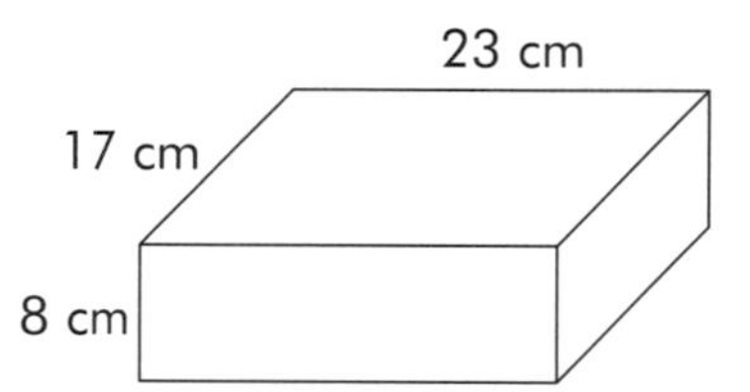

Volume =

13.

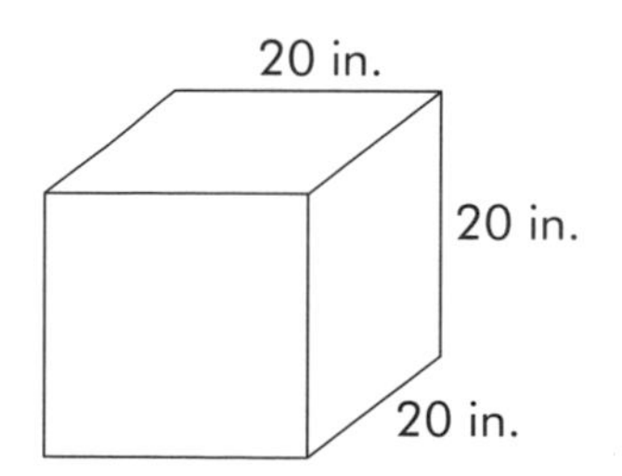

Volume =

Find the unknown.

14.

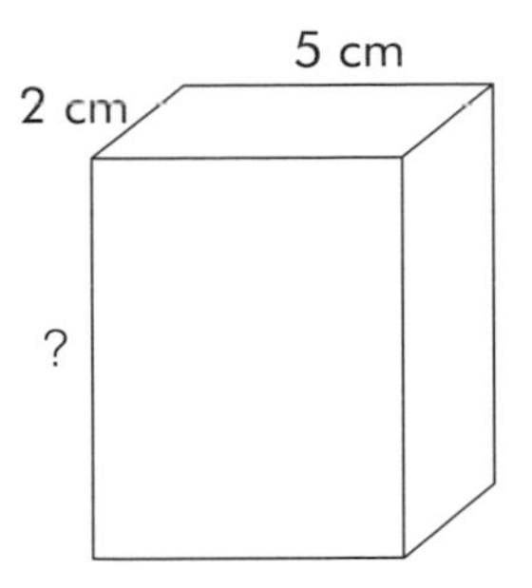

Find the height if the volume of the solid is 130 cm^3.

15.

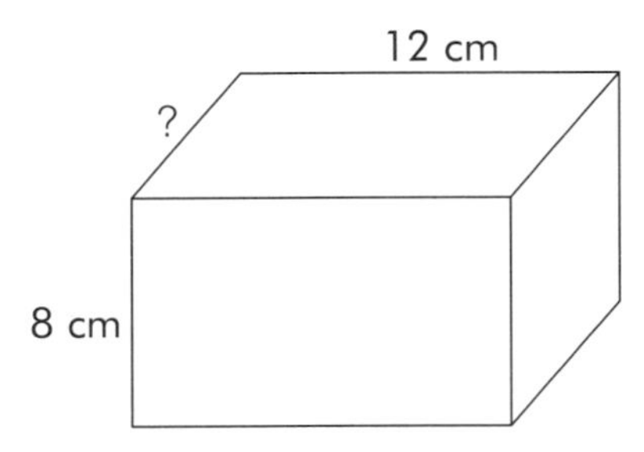

Find the width if the volume of the solid is 480 cm^3.

16.

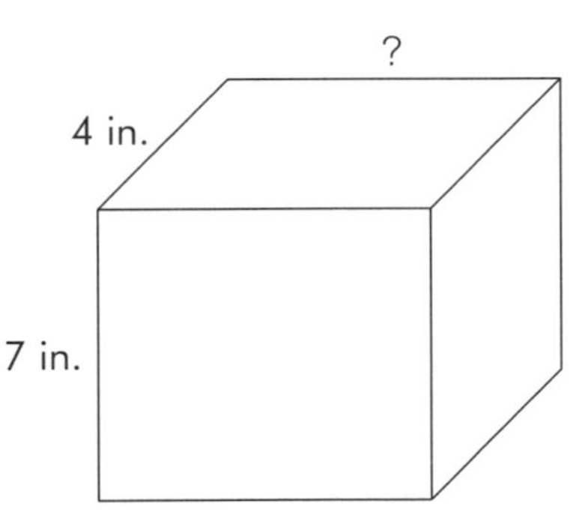

Find the length if the volume of the solid is 224 in.^{3}.

Write your answers on the lines. You may use a calculator whenever you see **.**

17. The solid below is made up of a cube and a rectangular block. The edge of the cube measures 12 cm. The rectangular block is similar to the cube except that its height is twice the edge of the cube. Find the volume of the solid.

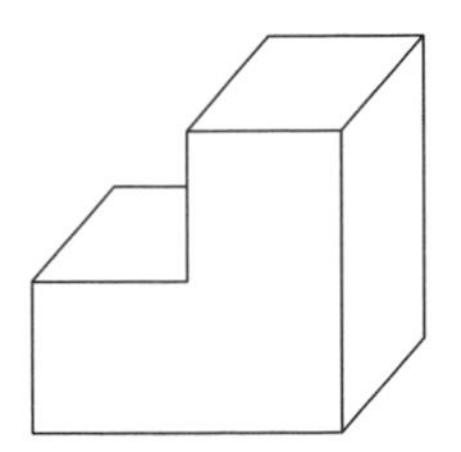

____

18. The volume of a cube is 2,197 in.^{3}. What is the length of each edge?

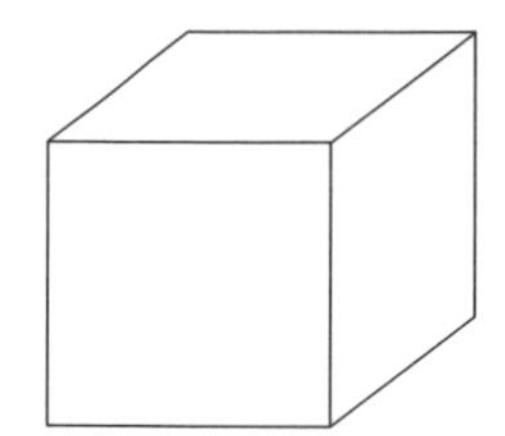

____

19. The volume of a rectangular prism is 4,224 cm^3. The area of the shaded face is 176 cm^2. Find its height.

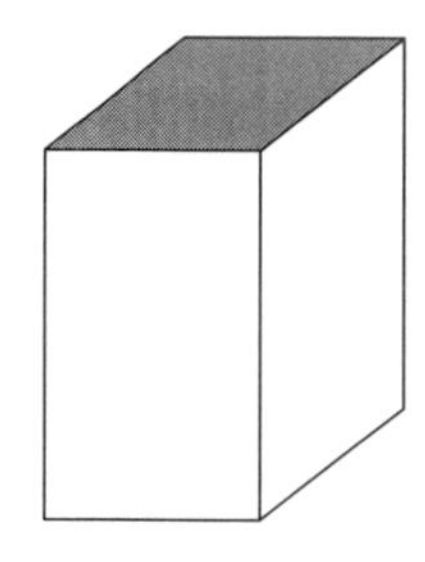

____

20. A rectangular block is cut from a solid 30 cm long, 13 cm wide, and 8 cm high. Find the volume of the remaining solid.

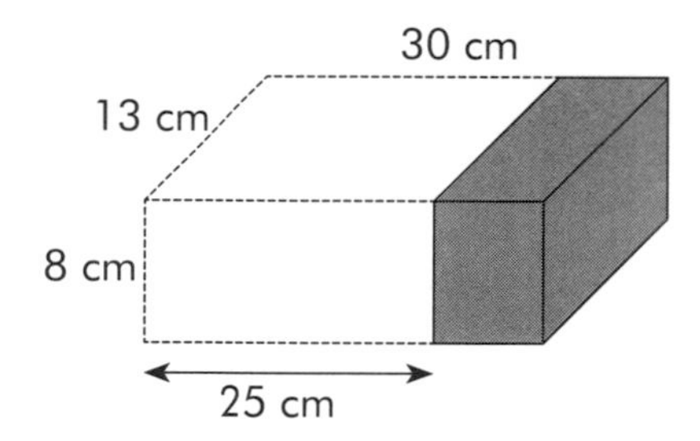

____

21. Four rows of cubes are stacked as shown below. The edge of each cube measures 4 in. If two rows of cubes are removed, find the volume of the remaining cubes.

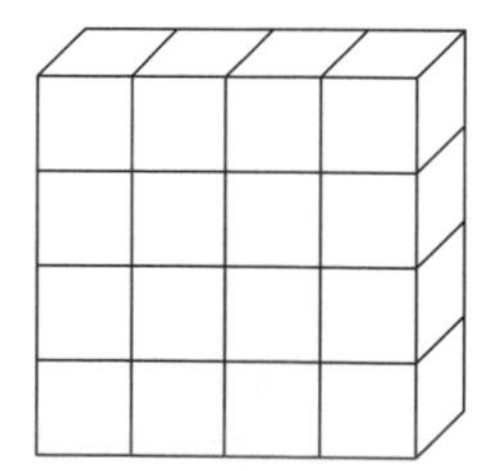

____

22. Rodolfo cut a hole in a rectangular prism measuring 32 cm by 28 cm by 4 cm. After cutting the hole, the rectangular prism became a frame with a border of 4 cm. Find the volume of the frame.

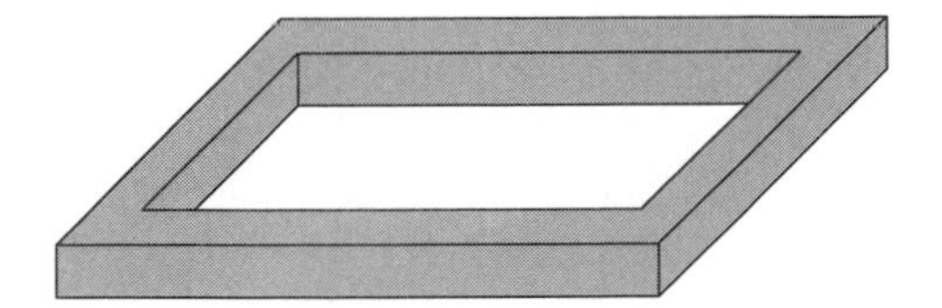

____

23. A tank measuring 55 cm by 22 cm by 40 cm is $\frac{3}{4}$ full of water. Find the volume of water in the tank. Express your answer in liters. (1 L = 1,000 cm^3)

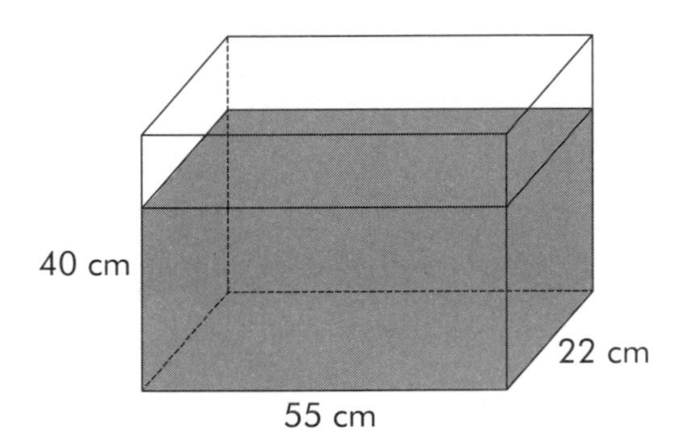

____

24. A rectangular vase measuring 15 cm by 12 cm by 50 cm is $\frac{1}{5}$ filled with water. Find the volume of water needed to fill the vase to its brim. Write your answer in liters and milliliters.
(1 L = 1,000 cm^3)

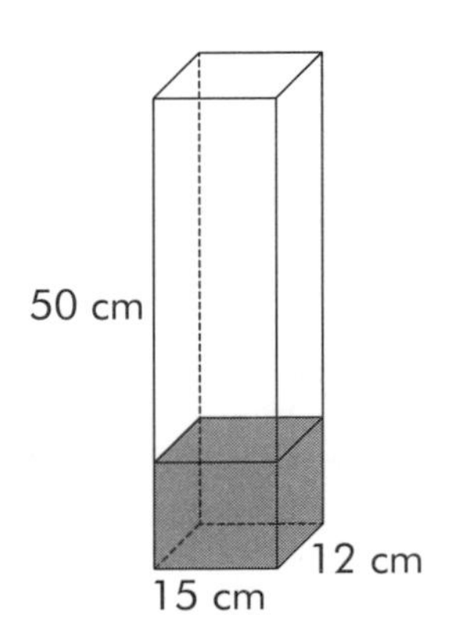

____

25. A rectangular tank has a base measuring 36 cm by 26 cm. It is half-filled with water. What is the height of the tank if the volume of water in the tank is 11,232 cm^3?

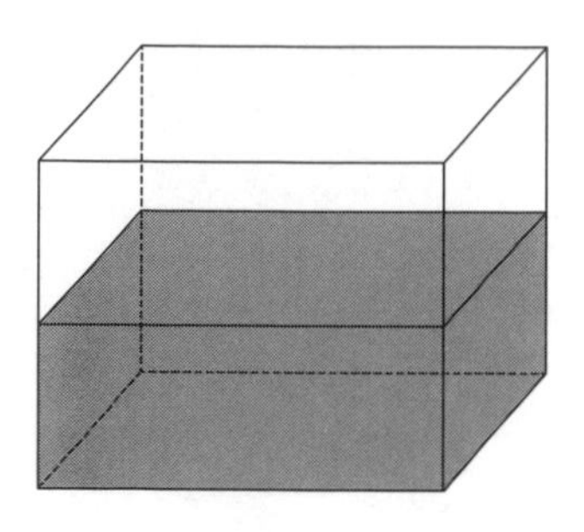

____

26. A tank measuring 100 cm by 330 cm by 80 cm is completely filled with water. How long will it take for the water in the tank to be completely drained at 11 liters per minute? Write your answer in minutes. (1 L = 1,000 cm^3)

____

27. The volume of a rectangular prism is 24,300 cm^3. Its base area is 1,350 cm^2. Find its length when its height is $\frac{2}{5}$ the length of the rectangular prism.

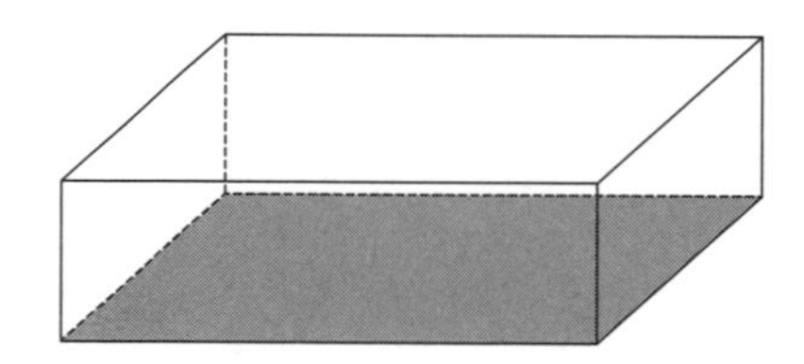

____

28. A metal ball with a volume of 576 $in.^3$ is melted and molded into nine identical cubes. What is the edge of each cube?

____

29. A rectangular fish tank with a base measuring 35 cm by 60 cm contains 63 L of water when it is $\frac{3}{4}$ full. What is the height of the rectangular fish tank? (1 L = 1,000 cm^3)

____

30. The base of a rectangular solid measures 16 cm by 6 cm. If the rectangular solid has the same volume as a 12-cm cube, what is the height of the rectangular solid?

____

31. The volume of a cubical tank is 6,859 cm^3. Find the base area of the cubical tank.

____

32. A tank can hold 1.65 L of water when it is $\frac{3}{5}$ full of water. Find the area of its base, given the height of the tank is 22 cm. (1 L = 1,000 cm^3)

____

33. A tank measuring 35 cm by 22 cm by 38 cm is $\frac{3}{4}$ full of water. 11.935 L of water are poured out of the tank. Find the height of the water left in the tank. (1 L = 1,000 cm^3)

____

34. A container measuring 56 cm by 50 cm by 60 cm is being filled with water flowing from a tap at a rate of 12 liters per minute. How long does it take to fill the container completely with water? (1 L = 1,000 cm^3)

____

Solve the following story problems. Show your work in the space below.

35. A rectangular container measuring 40 cm by 45 cm by 55 cm is filled with water to its brim.

    (a) What is the capacity of the container? Write your answer in liters.

    (b) If a tap is used to drain water from the container at a rate of 11 liters per minute, how long will it take to drain all the water from the container?

    (1 L = 1,000 cm^3)

36. A rectangular prism measuring 20 in. by 24 in. by 40 in. is cut into 300 cubes of the same size. Find the edge of each cube.

37. Jack cut a hole measuring 20 cm by 10 cm by 27 cm from a rectangular prism 24 cm long, 14 cm wide and 27 cm high. Find the volume of the remaining rectangular prism.

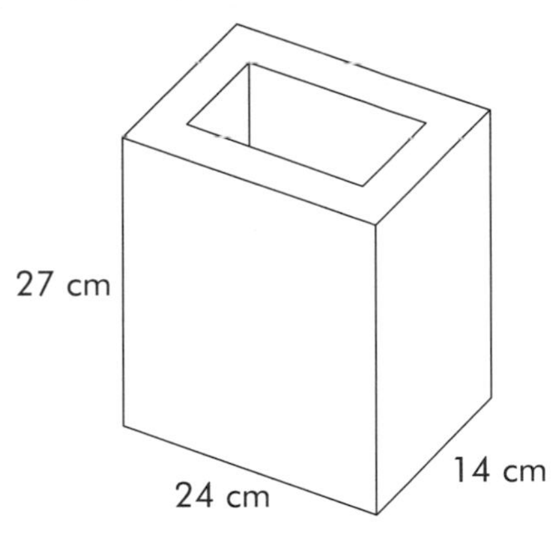

38. A rectangular tank measuring 16 in. by 15 in. by 20 in. is completely filled with water. The water is then poured into an empty cubical tank with an edge of 20 in. What is the height of the water in the cubical tank?

39. A rectangular water tank is 80 cm long, 60 cm wide, and 1 m high. A tap is turned on to fill the tank completely with water. How long will it take to fill the tank completely if the water flows at a rate of 4.8 L per minute?
(1 L = 1,000 cm^3)

40. Water was flowing into a large empty aquarium from a tap at a rate of 32 liters per minute. 30 minutes later, another tap was turned on, and water flowed into the aquarium from the second tap at a rate of 40 liters per minute. Both taps were turned off $2\frac{1}{2}$ hours after the second tap was turned on. If the aquarium measured 320 cm by 150 cm, what was the height of the water in it?
(1 L = 1,000 cm^3)

Unit 12: CHALLENGING WORD PROBLEMS

Example:

Francis has a total of \$15.75 in nickels and quarters. $\frac{1}{4}$ of his coins are nickels. How many coins of each type did he have?

nickels	quarters	quarters	quarters

\$15.75

Use the Guess-and-Check method.

Number of quarters	Number of nickels	Total amount
20	5	$(20 \times \$0.25) + (5 \times \$0.05) = \$5.25$
40	10	$(40 \times \$0.25) + (10 \times \$0.05) = \$10.50$
60	15	$(60 \times \$0.25) + (15 \times \$0.05) = \$15.75$

He has <u>60</u> quarters and <u>15</u> nickels.

Solve the following story problems. Show your work in the space below.

1. David drove at an average rate of speed of 33 mph for the first $1\frac{1}{2}$ hr. of his trip. He then doubled his rate of speed for the next $1\frac{3}{4}$ hr. David slowed down to 60 mph for the remaining $\frac{1}{2}$ hr. of his journey. Find David's average rate of speed for the whole trip.

2. Jerry, Wendy, and Carmen were given some raffle tickets to sell. Each ticket was sold for $5. Jerry sold $\frac{3}{7}$ of the tickets. Wendy sold $\frac{1}{3}$ of what Carmen sold. If Wendy sold 60 fewer tickets than Jerry, how much money did they collect altogether?

3. Sunee had 3 times as many dimes as pennies. She had 5 times as many quarters as dimes. If she had $64.96 in all, how many dimes did she have?

4. A driver, traveling at a constant rate of speed of 55 mph, passed Town A at 6:15 P.M. He reached Town B at 9:45 P.M. A motorcyclist, traveling at a constant rate of speed of 62 mph, passed Town A and reached Town B at the same time as the driver. At what time did the motorcyclist pass Town A?

5. Town X and Town Y are 560 km apart. At 11 A.M., a van leaves Town X for Town Y, traveling at a constant rate of speed. At the same time, a bus leaves for Town Y from Town X, also traveling at a constant rate of speed. The two vehicles pass each other at 1:20 P.M. The average rate of speed of the van is 60 km/h faster than the bus.

   (a) Find the van's average rate of speed.

   (b) How far is the bus from Town X when it passes the van?

6. Sanjiv bought a laptop at a discount of 25%. He increased the price of the laptop by 25% and sold it to Kenny. Kenny spent $150 on repairs, increased its price by 8%, and sold it to Perry. If Perry paid $1,377 for the laptop,

   (a) at what price did Sanjiv buy the laptop?

   (b) what was the original price of the laptop?

7. 4 pairs of jeans and 5 T-shirts cost $129.10. 5 pairs of jeans and 4 T-shirts cost $139.10. Find the cost of a pair of jeans and a T-shirt.

8. Brenda had some flower seeds. If she gave each friend 8 seeds, she would need another 44 seeds. If she gave each friend 16 seeds, she would need another 220 seeds. How many friends did she give the seeds to?

9. Lorraine bought some stationery. The ratio of pens to pencils to erasers was 6:13:4. She then gave away some pens and pencils. The ratio of pens to pencils to erasers left was 4:17:7. If Lorraine had 91 pencils at first, how many pens and pencils did she give away?

10. Mrs. Lyons bought some chocolate and lollipops in the ratio 7:4. The price of all the chocolate to the price of all lollipops was in the ratio 5:2. She spent $127.40 in all. If each lollipop cost 15¢ less than each chocolate, how many lollipops did she buy?

REVIEW 3

Choose the correct answer, and write its number in the parentheses. You may use a calculator whenever you see 🖩**.**

The pie chart below shows the favorite holiday destinations listed by a class of 40 students. Study it carefully, and answer questions 1 to 2.

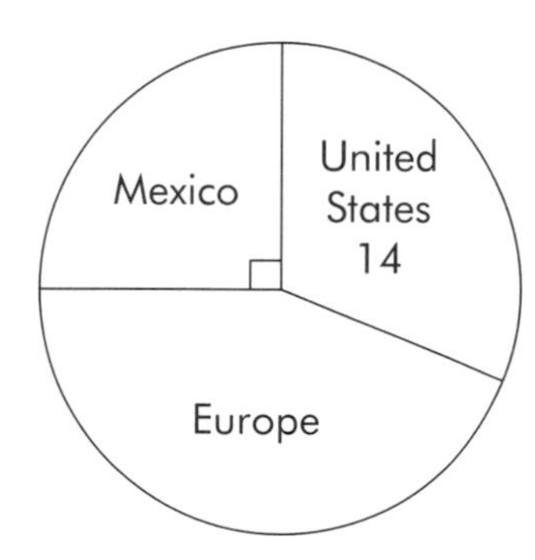

1. How many students want to visit Mexico?

   (1) 10 (3) 26
   (2) 16 (4) 30 ( )

2. How many more students want to visit Europe than the United States?

   (1) 2 (3) 6
   (2) 4 (4) 10 ( )

3. A can of corn has a circular cover of diameter 30 cm. What is the area of the circular cover? (Use $\pi = 3.14$)

   (1) 94.2 cm^2 (3) 706.5 cm^2
   (2) 188.4 cm^2 (4) 2826 cm^2 ( )

4. The base of a fish tank measures 32 in. by 28 in. Its volume is 10,880 $in.^3$ when it is $\frac{5}{7}$ full of water. Find the height of the fish tank.

   (1) 17 in. (3) 20 in.
   (2) 19 in. (4) 21 in. ( )

5. The figure below shows a quadrant and a semicircle. Find the area of the shaded part.

(Use $\pi = \frac{22}{7}$)

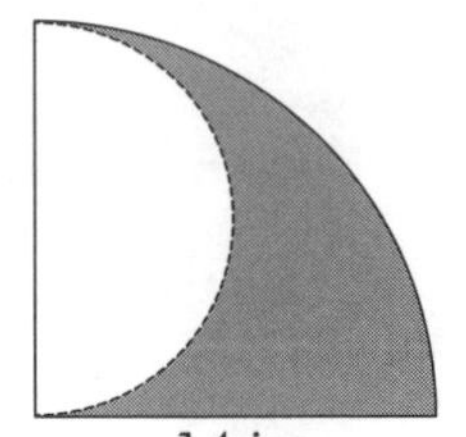

(1) 77 in.^{2}
(2) 154 in.^{2}
(3) 231 in.^{2}
(4) 616 in.^{2}

( )

6. An empty tank has a base area of 480 cm^2. Water from a tap flows into the tank at a rate of 5 liters per minute. Find the height of the water in the tank after 6 minutes.

(1 L = 1,000 cm^3)

(1) 31.25 cm
(2) 62.5 cm
(3) 80 cm
(4) 96 cm

( )

7. The figure below is made up of a rectangle and a square with an area of 64 cm^2. What is its perimeter?

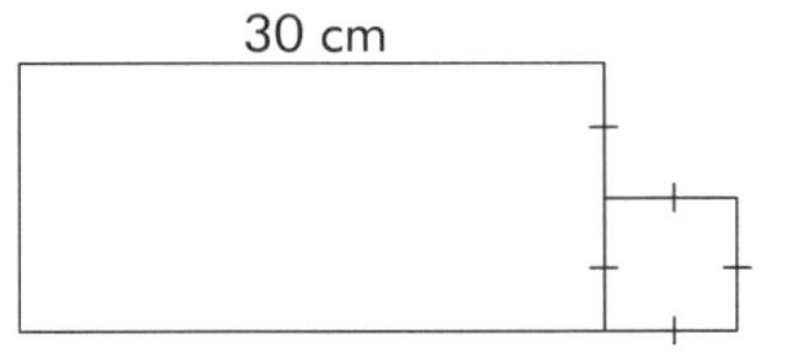

(1) 108 cm
(2) 116 cm
(3) 124 cm
(4) 156 cm

( )

Write your answers on the lines.

8. A container measuring 21 in. by 18 in. by 20 in. is $\frac{1}{5}$ full of water. How much water is needed to fill half of the container?

____

9. Find the circumference of a quadrant in a circle with a diameter of 56 in. (Use $\pi = \frac{22}{7}$)

____

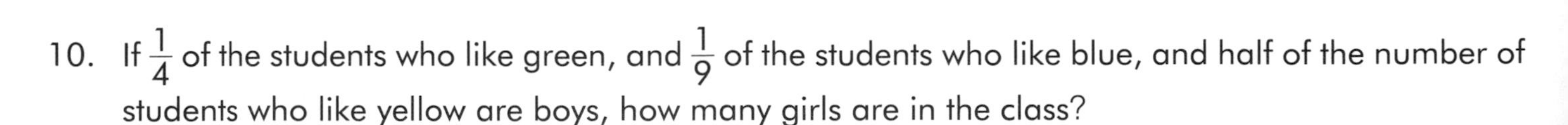

10. If $\frac{1}{4}$ of the students who like green, and $\frac{1}{9}$ of the students who like blue, and half of the number of students who like yellow are boys, how many girls are in the class?

____

11. The base of a triangle is 5 in. and its height is 10 in. The triangle has the same area as a square. Find the perimeter of the square.

____

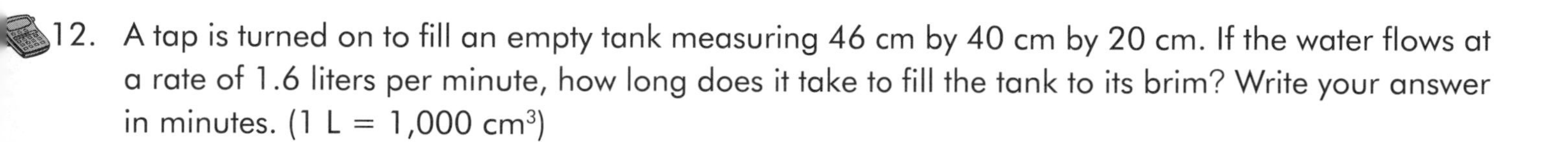

12. A tap is turned on to fill an empty tank measuring 46 cm by 40 cm by 20 cm. If the water flows at a rate of 1.6 liters per minute, how long does it take to fill the tank to its brim? Write your answer in minutes. (1 L = 1,000 cm^3)

____

13. The figure below is made up of two identical squares with 7 in. sides. What is the area of the shaded region?

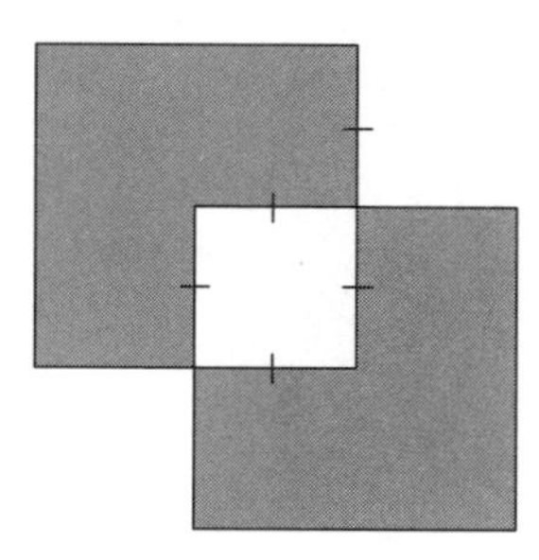

____

14. When a tank is completely filled with water, its capacity is 3 liters. Find the height of the tank when it has a base area of 300 cm^2. (1 L = 1,000 cm^3)

____

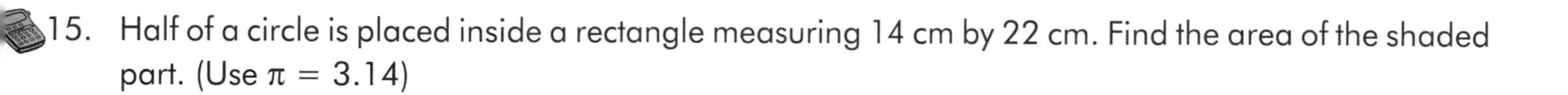

15. Half of a circle is placed inside a rectangle measuring 14 cm by 22 cm. Find the area of the shaded part. (Use $\pi = 3.14$)

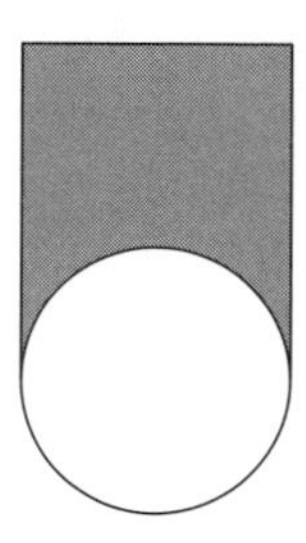

____

Solve the following story problems. Show your work in the space below.

16. The figure below is made up of two identical triangles. The base of the triangle is 36 in. and its height is 30 in. Find the area of each small triangle if the shaded area is 720 $in.^2$.

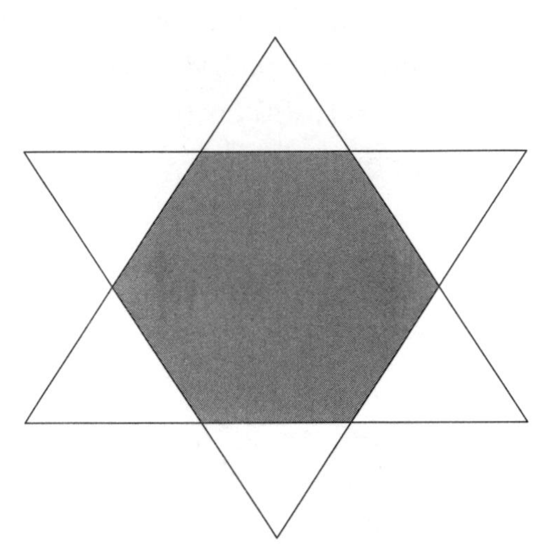

17. Six similar cubes are stacked as shown below. The total area of the shaded part is 600 cm^2. Find the volume of each cube.

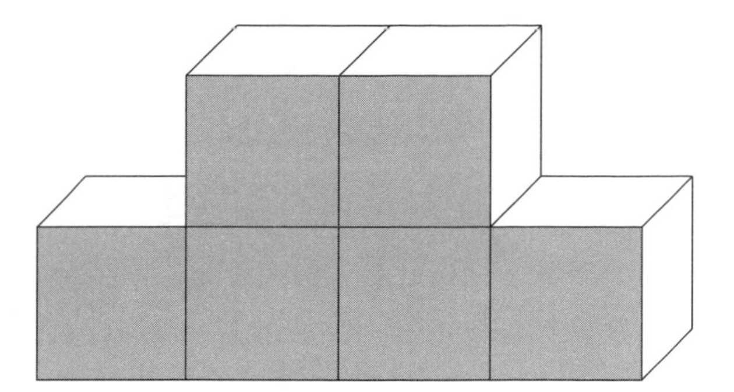

18. George set off at 12 noon, driving at a speed of 80 km/h and reached his destination at 10 P.M. Calvin set off the same time as George and reached the same destination 2 hours earlier than George. How far was George from his destination when he was 120 km apart from Calvin?

19. Rey and Omar shared some stamps. $\frac{1}{5}$ of Omar's stamps were $\frac{1}{3}$ of Rey's stamps. If Rey gave Omar 24 stamps, Omar would have three times as many stamps as Rey. Find the number of stamps each of them had in the beginning.

20. Four pens and three pencils cost \$18. Four rulers and three pencils cost \$12. The cost of three pens and three rulers is \$13.50. Find the cost of each pencil.

FINAL REVIEW

Choose the correct answer, and write its number in the parentheses.

1. Which of the following is the lowest common multiple of 9 and 12?

   (1) 3 (3) 72
   (2) 36 (4) 108 ( )

2. Calculate 45% of 9.

   (1) 0.405 (3) 4.05
   (2) 0.45 (4) 4.5 ( )

3. Calculate $3x + x^2$ when $x = 7$.

   (1) 21 (3) 49
   (2) 35 (4) 70 ( )

4. How many different ways can the figure shown below be divided into two equal parts?

   (1) 1
   (2) 2
   (3) 3
   (4) 4

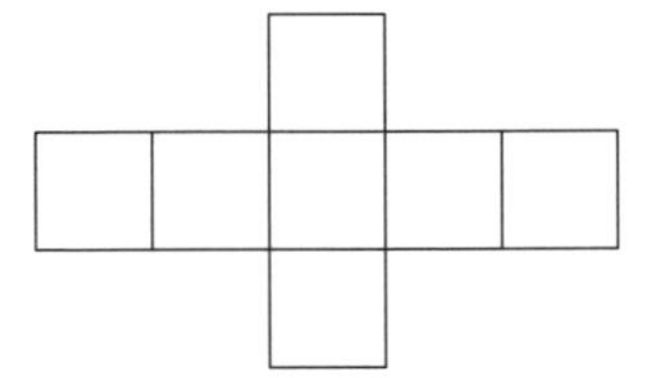

( )

5. What is the area of the shaded part?

   (1) 36 in.^{2}
   (2) 48 in.^{2}
   (3) 84 in.^{2}
   (4) 120 in.^{2}

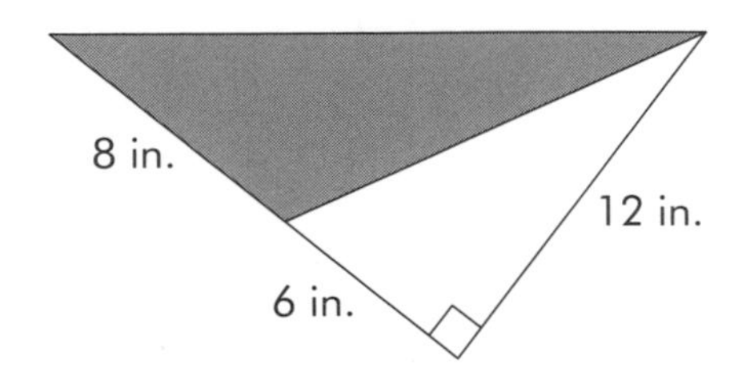

( )

6. The length of a ribbon is w cm. It is cut into two pieces. One piece is shorter than the other by 3 cm. Find the length of the longer piece in terms of w.

(1) $\left(\frac{w-3}{2}+3\right)$ cm
(2) $\left(\frac{w+3}{2}-3\right)$ cm
(3) $\left(\frac{w}{2}-3\right)$ cm
(4) $\left(\frac{w}{2}+3\right)$ cm ( )

7. ABCD is a square. 5 out of 6 identical rectangles in the smaller square have been shaded. How many more similar rectangles must be shaded so that $\frac{3}{8}$ of square ABCD is shaded?

(1) 3
(2) 4
(3) 9
(4) 24

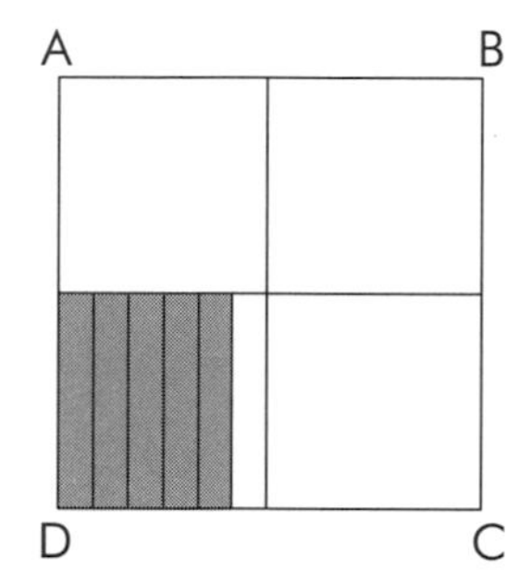

( )

8. Jamal was given 0.25 L of cough medicine. He took the cough medicine 4 times a day. If he took 15 mL of cough medicine each time, how much cough medicine did he have left after 3 days?

(1) 60 mL
(2) 70 mL
(3) 180 mL
(4) 250 mL ( )

9. The figure below is made up of rectangle and squares. Find the perimeter of the figure in terms of x.

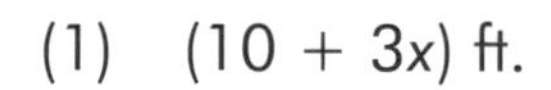

(1) $(10 + 3x)$ ft.
(2) $(15 + 6x)$ ft.
(3) $(15 + 8x)$ ft.
(4) $(20 + 6x)$ ft.

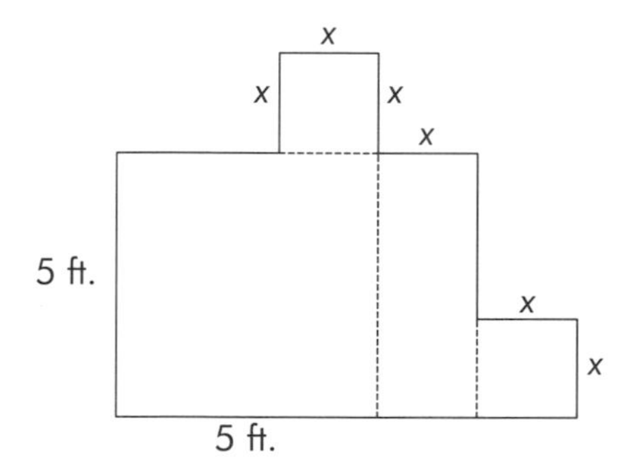

( )

10. Which two shapes cannot be drawn as a tessellation?

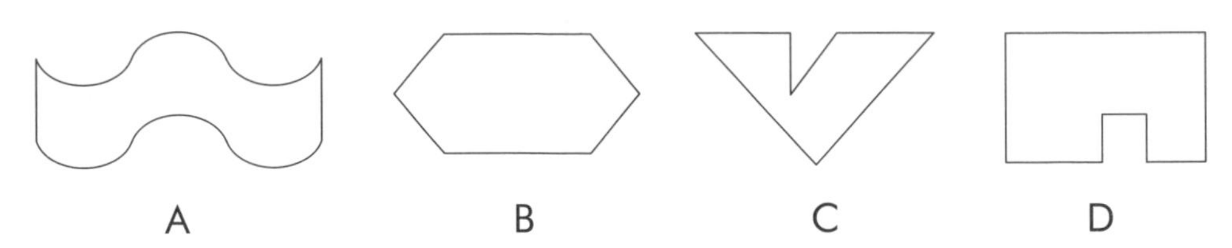

(1) A and B
(2) B and C
(3) C and D
(4) D and A
( )

11. How much more water is needed to fill completely the tank below?

(1) 2,640 cm^3
(2) 3,360 cm^3
(3) 3,520 cm^3
(4) 6,160 cm^3

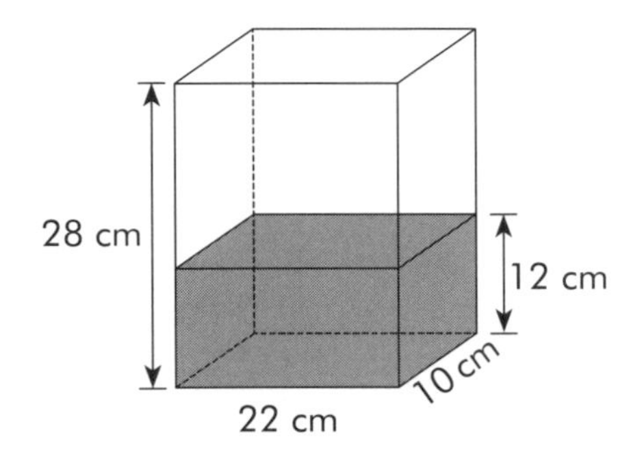

( )

12. The circumference of a semicircle is 110 in. What is its radius? (Use $\pi = \frac{22}{7}$)

(1) 17.5 in.
(2) 27.5 in.
(3) 35 in.
(4) 70 in.
( )

13. A tank had a base area of 26 in. by 19 in. When the water level increased by 8 in., the volume of water in the tank became 8,892 $in.^3$. What was the original height of the water in the tank?

(1) 10 in.
(2) 14 in.
(3) 16 in.
(4) 18 in.
( )

14. In the figure shown below, the area of the rectangle is 480 $yd.^2$. What is the perimeter of the figure? (Use $\pi = 3.14$)

(1) 31.4 yd.
(2) 68 yd.
(3) 95.4 yd.
(4) 99.4 yd.

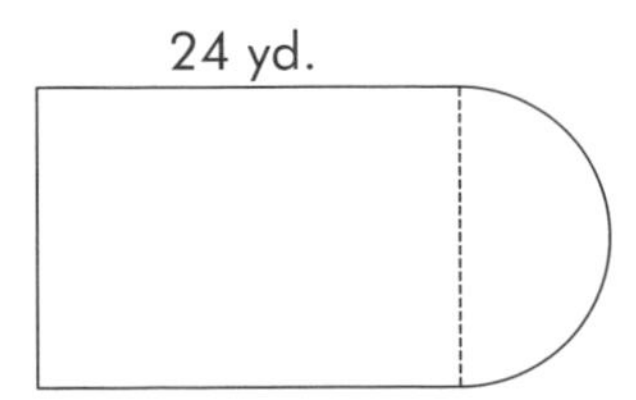

( )

15. Calculate $45 \times (2 + 7) - 105 \div 5$.

(1) 60 (3) 300

(2) 76 (4) 384 ( )

Write your answers on the lines.

The pie chart below shows the number of people attending a concert. Study it carefully, and answer questions 16 and 17.

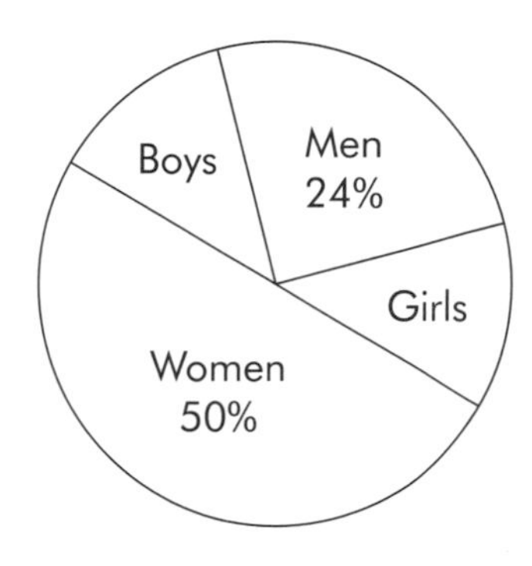

16. There were as many boys as girls at the concert. What percentage of the audience were girls?

____

17. If there were 264 men at the concert, how many people attended the concert?

____

18. In the figure below, AOB and COD are straight lines. Find $\angle x$.

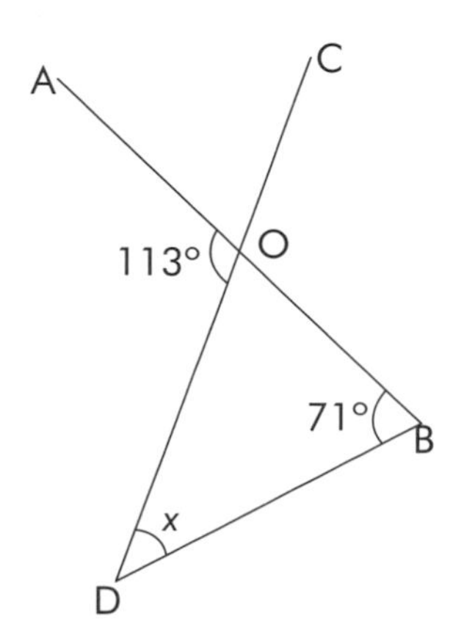

____

19. Shade 2 squares to make the figure below symmetrical.

20. Mrs. Ivankovic sold 280 cups of tea on Friday and $2\frac{4}{7}$ times as many cups of tea on Saturday. If each cup of tea costs $0.75, how much money did she collect from the sale of tea on these two days?

____

21. The container below has a capacity of 1,008 cm^3 and a base area of 56 cm^2. What is the height of water in the container when it is $\frac{7}{9}$ full?

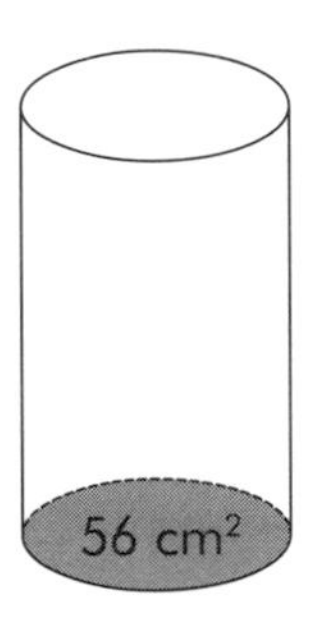

____

22. In the figure below, a shape is formed when you draw 1.25 in. around point Z. What is the shape?

•Z

____

23. The figure below shows a cube and its net. Mark on the net with a cross where x is supposed to be.

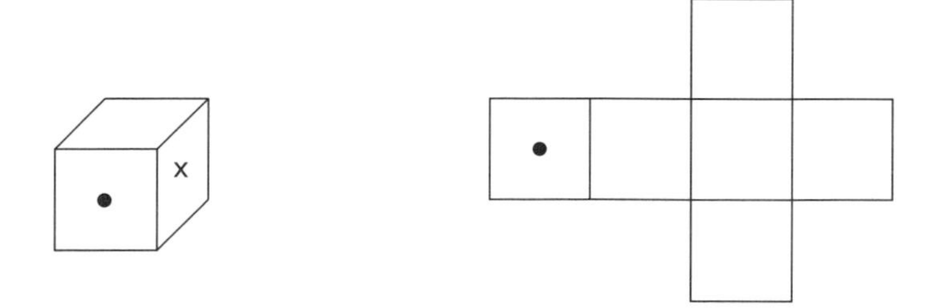

24. Cedric has an equal number of dimes and nickels with a total value of $10.50. How many coins does he have in all?

____

25. What is the maximum number of 2-in. cubes that can be put into a rectangular box measuring 24 in. by 20 in. by 36 in.?

____

26. In the figure below, a circle is enclosed in a square with a side of 28 cm. Find the ratio of the area of the circle to that of the square. (Use $\pi = \frac{22}{7}$)

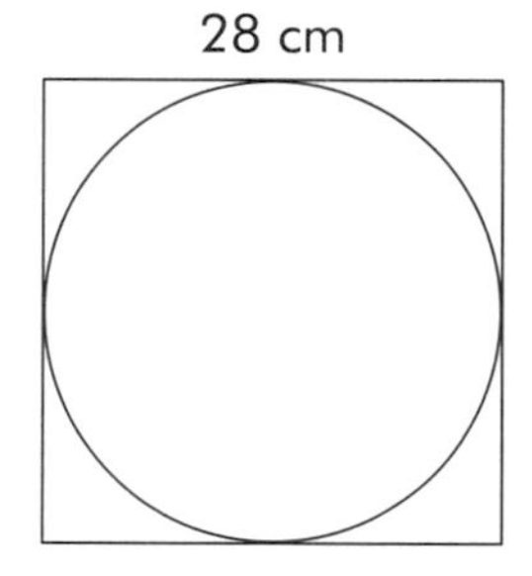

____

27. Belinda made a 4 cm by 6 cm by 6 cm rectangular prism using 2-cm cubes. She removed some cubes to make the solid as shown below. How many cubes did she remove?

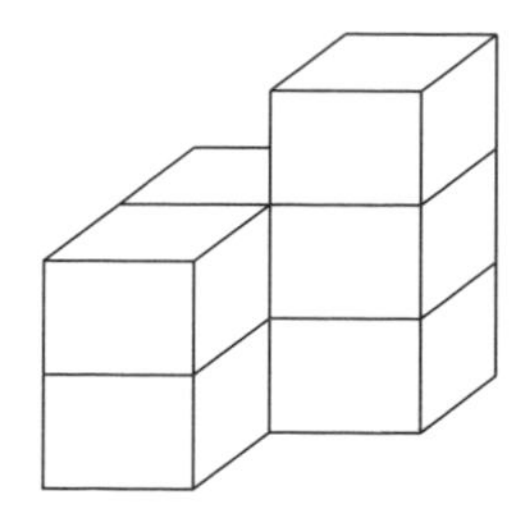

____

28. What is the correct value indicated by the arrow?

29. Pam left her office at 5:45 P.M. and reached home at 7:15 P.M. How long was her trip home?

30. Peter faces northwest after turning 225° clockwise. Which direction was he facing at first?

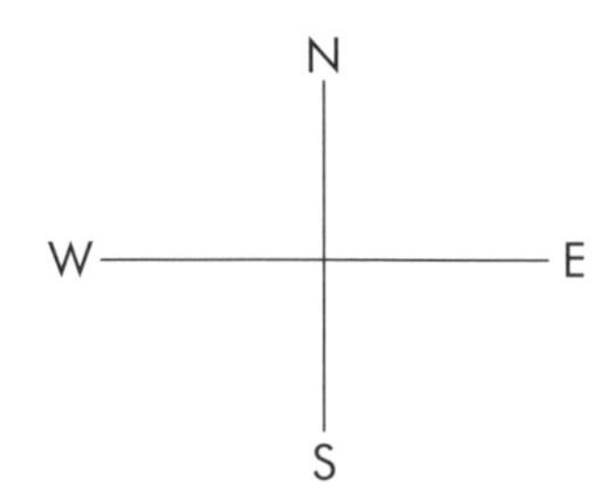

Write your answers on the lines. You may use a calculator.

31. How many tenths are there in 309.4?

32. A rope $20\frac{3}{4}$ ft. long is cut into 6 equal pieces. What is the length of each piece? Write your answer as a decimal to the nearest tenth.

33. What percentage of the figure below is shaded?

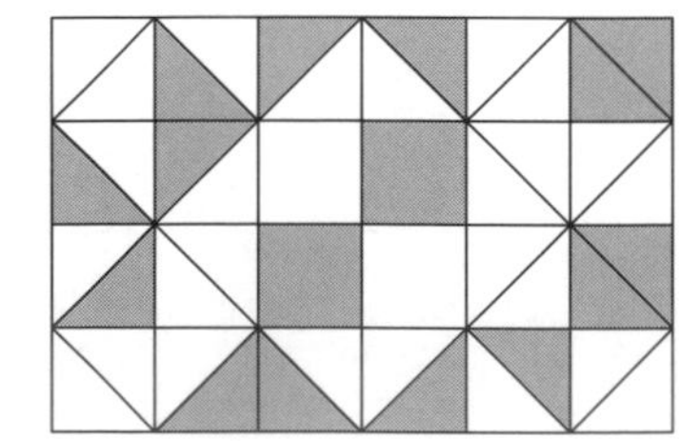

34. Multiply 23 tens by 51 hundredths. ____________

35. Arrange the following numbers in ascending order.

$$\frac{23}{5},\ 6.4,\ 0.46,\ \frac{16}{25}$$

____

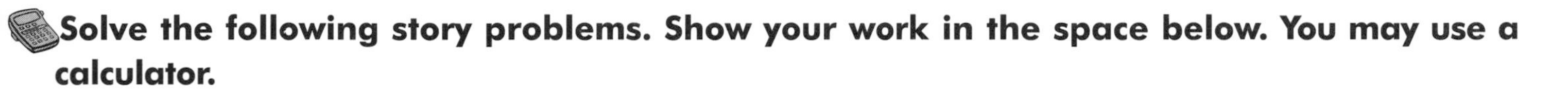

Solve the following story problems. Show your work in the space below. You may use a calculator.

36. The total mass of a dozen apples is 3.187 kg. The total mass of 15 apples is 4 kg. Find the average mass of 3 apples. Write your answer in grams.

37. 24 trees along a highway are planted at an equal distance from each other. If the distance between the first tree and the last tree is 74.52 yd., what is the distance between the fifth tree and the ninth tree?

38. The figure below is not drawn to scale. ABCD is a parallelogram and ABE is a triangle.

(a) Find $\angle AEB$.

(b) Find $\angle AFD$.

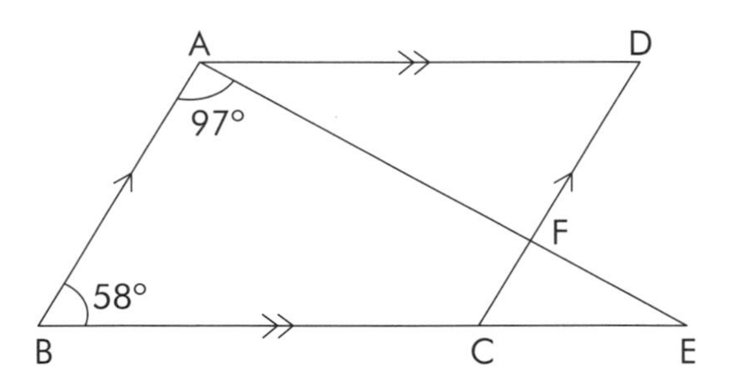

39. A hamburger costs $\$(5x + 3)$ and a drink costs $\$2x$ less. Andre and his two brothers used an equal amount of money to buy three hamburgers and two drinks. How much did each boy have to pay? Write your answer in terms of x.

40. Patrick drove from Town X to Town Y. He completed $\frac{3}{5}$ of the trip in two hours. The average rate of speed for the two hours was 45 mph. He completed the rest of the trip in another hour.

    (a) Find the total distance between Town X and Town Y.

    (b) Find Patrick's average rate of speed for the whole trip.

41. 6 bricks measuring 12 cm by 10 cm by 8 cm each were placed in an empty tank. Water was then poured into the tank until it reached a height of 20 cm. The ratio of the volume of water in the tank to the volume of the 6 bricks was 9:8. If the base of the tank was square in shape, find its length.

42. The solid below is formed by two cubes. If the total volume of the solid is 728 cm^3, what is the difference between the base area of cube A and the base area of cube B?

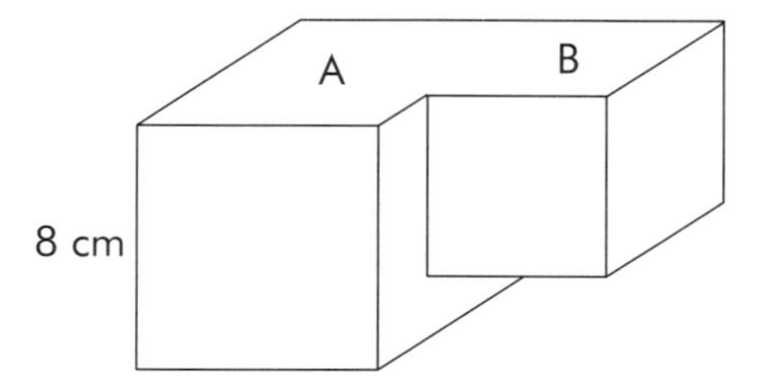

43. The ratio of red beads to blue beads in a box was 7:4. When 81 red beads were used to make a necklace, the ratio of blue beads to red beads became 10:13.

(a) How many beads were there at first?

(b) How many more red beads than blue beads were there in the end?

44. The incomplete table below shows the charges of water usage in Acme Town.

Category	Quantity	Charges per m^3
A	First 10 m^3	
B	Next 10 m^3	\$0.85
C	After 20 m^3	

(a) The charges of water usage in Category A is 20% less than that of Category B. The charges of water usage in Category C is 50% more than that of Category A. Complete the above table.

(b) If a family had to pay \$32.64 for the water usage in the month of May, how much water did the family use in May?

45. The figure below is made up of a triangle, and a semicircle enclosed in a rectangle. The width of the rectangle is 210 in. Its length is $\frac{1}{3}$ longer than its width. Find the area of the shaded portion. (Use $\pi = \frac{22}{7}$)

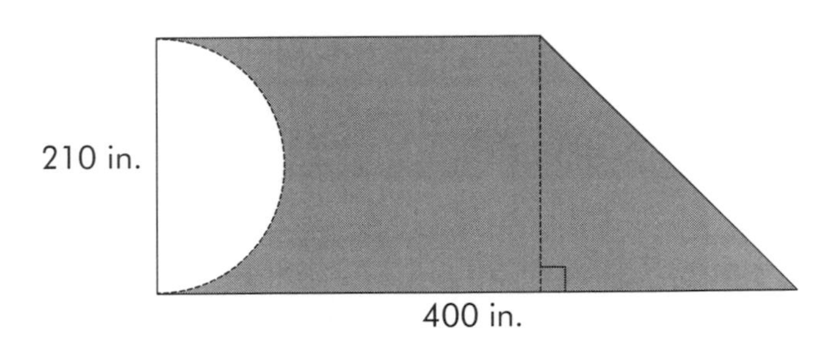

46. ABCD is a square of side 35 cm. Find the area of the shaded part.

(Use $\pi = \frac{22}{7}$)

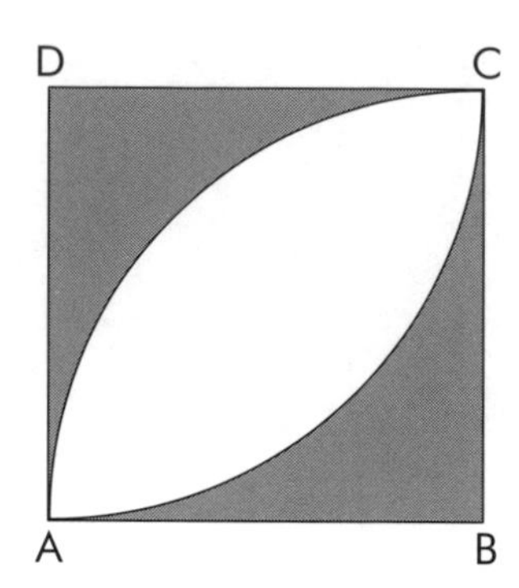

47. Gina and Barry shared $980. Gina received 2.5 times as much money as Barry. Then, Gina's dad gave her some money, and Barry got some money from his grandmother. For every $7 Barry had, his grandmother gave him $20. The amount of money that Gina had in the end was $\frac{7}{9}$ of the amount of money Barry had in the end. Write the amount of money that Gina received from her father as a fraction of the amount of money Barry received from his grandmother.

48. The figure below is made up of 3 semicircles. The biggest semicircle covers parts of the two smaller semicircles. Find the shaded area of the figure.
(Use $\pi = 3.14$)

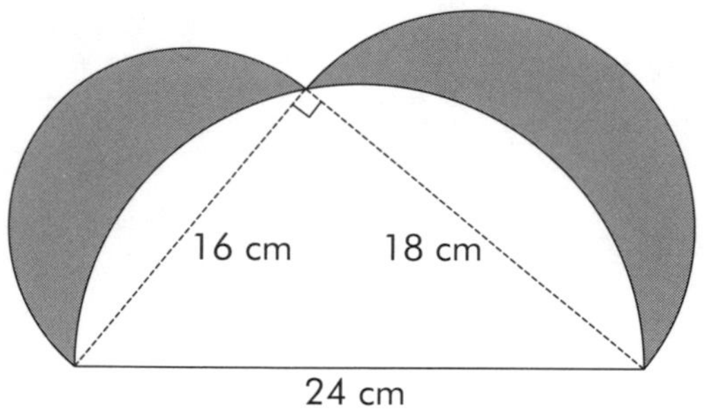

16 cm
18 cm
24 cm

CHALLENGE QUESTIONS

Solve the following problems on another sheet of paper.

1. Ming, Betsy, and Christine have some money. The amount of money that Ming and Betsy have is $85. The amount of money that Betsy and Christine have is $100. The amount of money that Christine and Ming have is $81. How much does each of them have?

2. 10 people can sit around a rectangular table for a meal. When two tables are joined side by side, 18 people can sit around the two tables. When three tables are joined side by side, 26 people can sit around the three tables. How many rectangular tables are needed for 90 people to sit around?

3. I am a 2-digit number. My first digit is 1.5 times more than the second digit. Both the digits are factors of 24. The sum of both digits is an even number. What am I?

4. In a group, some children like swimming, while others like skiing or both sports. 25 children like swimming, and 21 children like skiing. Of these, 13 like both swimming and skiing. How many children are there in the group?

5. The sum of number A and number B is 29. Their product is 210. Find the two numbers.

6. In recent years, the number of tourists visiting Egypt tripled every half a year. If there were 4,455 tourists visiting Egypt in December 2009, find the number of tourists who visited Egypt in June 2008.

7. 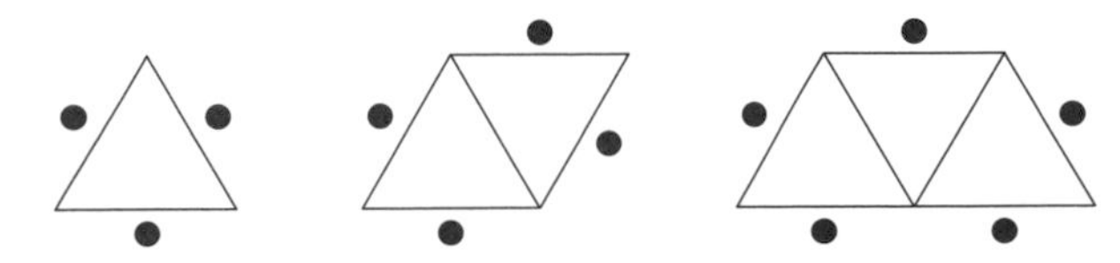

   3 people can sit around a triangular table. 4 people can sit around two tables. 5 people can sit around three tables. How many people can sit around 100 tables?

8. I am a 4-digit number.

   - The sum of all my digits is 10.
   - The sum of my first and third digits equals my last digit.
   - My third digit is 60% of the last digit.

   What am I?

9. Grace, Carlos, and Dalila have some stamps. The total number of Grace and Dalila's stamps is 219. The total number of Carlos and Dalila's stamps is 266. The total number of Grace and Carlos's stamps is 297. Find the number of stamps each child has.

10. At a learning center, some teachers teach English, while others teach mathematics or both subjects. 52 teachers teach English, and 38 teachers teach mathematics. Of these, 22 teachers teach both subjects. How many teachers are there in the learning center?

11. The value of an antique watch increases 4 times every 10 years. If the watch had a value of $8,590 in 1990, in which year would the watch have a value of $137,440?

12. The sum of Eduardo and George's age is 36. The product of their age is 320. Find the difference between their ages.

SOLUTIONS

Singapore Math Practice Level 6B

Unit 7: Rate

1. **550 yd. per min.**
2. **1 m/s**
3. **6 km**
4. **1 ft.**
5. **60 mi.**
6. **2 cm**

	Time	Distance	Rate
7.	2 hr.	194 mi.	Speed = Distance ÷ Time = 194 ÷ 2 = **97 mph**
8.	30 min.	Distance = Rate × Time = 116 × 30 = **3480 m**	116 m/min.
9.	Time = Distance ÷ Rate = 50 ÷ 10 = **5 sec.**	50 ft.	10 ft./sec.
10.	60 hr.	1,560 mi.	Rate = Distance ÷ Time = 1,560 ÷ 60 = **26 mph**
11.	Time = Distance ÷ Rate = 336 ÷ 8 = **42 min.**	336 m	8 m/min.
12.	2 sec.	Distance = Rate × Time = 14 × 2 = **28 cm**	14 cm/sec.
13.	19 hr.	988 mi.	Rate = Distance ÷ Time = 988 ÷ 19 = **52 mph**
14.	Time = Distance ÷ Rate = 1829 ÷ 59 = **31 sec.**	1,829 m	59 m/s
15.	67 min.	Distance = Rate × Time = 99 × 67 = **6,633 m**	99 m/min.
16.	48 sec.	768 ft.	Rate = Distance ÷ Time = 768 ÷ 48 = **16 ft./sec.**

17. **5 ft. per min.**
Total distance = 32 + 48 = 80 ft.
Total time = 9 + 7 = 16 min.
Total distance ÷ Total time = 80 ÷ 16 = 5 ft./min.

18. **41 cm/sec.**
Total distance = 372 + 243 = 615 cm
Total time = 8 + 7 = 15 sec.
Total distance ÷ Total time = 615 ÷ 15 = 41 cm/sec.

19. **17 mi. per min.**
Total distance = 150 + 630 + 240 = 1,020 mi.
Total time = 11 + 30 + 19 = 60 min.
Total distance ÷ Total time = 1020 ÷ 60 = 17 mi./min.

20. **32.5 ft. per min.**
Total distance = 461 + 239 + 1250 = 1,950 ft.
Total time = 18 + 7 + 35 = 60 min.
Total distance ÷ Total time = 1,950 ÷ 60 = 32.5 ft./min.

21. **39 km/min.**
Total distance = 603 + 894 + 375 = 1,872 km
Total time = 21 + 18 + 9 = 48 min.
Total distance ÷ Total time = 1,872 ÷ 48 = 39 km/min.

22. **220 km**
Distance = Rate × Time = 55 × 4 = 220 mi.

23. **6.5 h**
Time = Distance ÷ Rate = 416 ÷ 64 = 6.5 hr.

24. **24.5 m/min**
Rate = Distance ÷ Time = 580 ÷ 20 = 29 m/min.
$\frac{29 + 20}{2}$ = 24.5 m/min.

25. **50 mph**
Rate = Distance ÷ Time = 75 ÷ $1\frac{1}{2}$ = 50 mph

26. **360 km**
Distance = Rate × Time = 75 × $4\frac{4}{5}$ = 360 km

27. **13 mph**
Time = Distance ÷ Rate = 96 ÷ 16 = 6 min.
Distance = Rate × Time = 12 × 18 = 216 mi.
Average rate of speed = Total distance ÷ Total time
= (96 + 216) ÷ (6 + 18)
= 312 ÷ 24
= 13 mph

28. **11 sec.**
Time = Distance ÷ Rate = 2,046 ÷ 186 = 11 sec.

29. **24 mi.**
Distance = Rate × Time = 60 × $\frac{24}{60}$ = 24 mi.

30. **288 m**
Total distance = Rate × Time
= (8 × 12) + (12 × 16)
= 96 + 192
= 288 m

31. **227.5 mi.**
Total distance = Rate × Time
= $\left(60 \times 2\frac{2}{3}\right) + \left(45 \times 1\frac{1}{2}\right)$
= 160 + 67.5
= 227.5 mi.

32. Half an hour = $\frac{1}{2}$ × 60 = 30 min.
Rate = Distance ÷ Time = 540 ÷ 30 = 18 m/min.
Her average rate of speed is **18 m/min.**

33. Time = Distance ÷ Rate = 300 ÷ 60 = 5 hr.
He will take 5 hr. to reach St. Louis.
10:45 + 5 hr. = 3:45 P.M.
He will reach St. Louis at **3:45 P.M.**

34. $\frac{15}{60} = \frac{1}{4}$ hr.
Distance = Rate × Time = 82 × $\frac{1}{4}$ = 20.5 km
The distance between Mr. Suksod's house and the office is 20.5 km.
$\frac{10}{60} = \frac{1}{6}$ hr.
Rate = Distance ÷ Time = 20.5 ÷ $\frac{1}{6}$ = 123 km/h
Mr. Taylor's rate of speed is 123 km/h.
123 – 82 = 41 km/h
The difference in their rates of speed is **41 km/h.**

35. Time = Distance ÷ Rate = 4 ÷ 4.8 = 0.83 × 60
= 50 min.
Eileen took 50 min to complete a 4-km run.
Time = Distance ÷ Rate = 4 ÷ 6 = 0.67 × 60
= 40 min.
Sally took 40 min. to complete a 4-km run.
50 – 40 = 10 min.
Eileen took **10 min.** more than Sally to complete her run.

36. From 10 am to 2 P.M., it was 4 hours.
Distance = Rate × Time = 52 × 4 = 208 mi.
The distance between Town A and Town B was 208 mi.
Time = Distance ÷ Rate = 208 ÷ 40 = $5\frac{1}{5}$ hr.
= 5 hr. 12 min.
William took 5 hr. 12 min. to reach Town B.
1 hr. 25 min. earlier than 10 A.M. was 8:35 A.M.
5 hr. 12 min. after 8:35 A.M. was 1:47 P.M.
William would reach Town B at **1.47 P.M.**

37. Distance = Rate × Time = 72 × $2\frac{1}{3}$ = 168 km
$\frac{4}{9} \rightarrow$ 168 km
$\frac{1}{9} \rightarrow$ 168 ÷ 4 = 42 km
$\frac{9}{9} \rightarrow$ 9 × 42 = 378 km
The distance between Town X and Town Y was 378 km.
Rate = Distance ÷ Time = 378 ÷ $4\frac{1}{5}$ = 90 km/h
Jessica's average rate of speed was **90 km/h** if she took $4\frac{1}{5}$ hours to travel from Town X to Town Y.

38. From 8:20 A.M. to 9 A.M., it is 40 minutes.
$\frac{40}{60} = \frac{2}{3}$ hr.
Distance = Rate × Time = 42 × $\frac{2}{3}$ = 28 mi.
40 – 5 = 35 min.
Rate = Distance ÷ Time = 28 ÷ $\frac{35}{60}$ = 48 mph
Tara's average rate of speed should be **48 mph** if she leaves home 5 minutes later than usual but wants to reach her office at the same time.

39. (a) Distance = Rate × Time
= 98 × $1\frac{18}{60}$
= $127\frac{2}{5}$ km
The motorcyclist traveled $127\frac{2}{5}$ km in 1 hr. 18 min.
Distance = Rate × Time
= 82 × $1\frac{18}{60}$
= $106\frac{3}{5}$ km
The motorist traveled $106\frac{3}{5}$ km in 1 hr. 18 min.
$127\frac{2}{5} + 106\frac{3}{5}$ = 234 km
The distance between Town Y and Town Z is **234 km.**
(b) 234 – $106\frac{3}{5}$ = $127\frac{2}{5}$ km
The motorist had to travel **$127\frac{2}{5}$ km** in order to reach Town Y.

40. Distance = Rate × Time = 60 × $2\frac{1}{2}$ = 150 mi.
Ricky traveled 150 mi. in $2\frac{1}{2}$ hours.
$4\frac{1}{2} - 2\frac{1}{2} - \frac{1}{2} = 1\frac{1}{2}$ hr.
Distance = Rate × Time = 60 × $1\frac{1}{2}$ = 90 mi.
150 + 90 = 240 mi.
Town P was **240 mi.** away from Town Q.

41. (a) Use the Guess-and-Check method.

Time	Total distance traveled by Kumiko	Total distance traveled by Claudia
4:20 to 5 P.M. (40 min.)	108 × $\frac{40}{60}$ = 72 km	0
5 to 6 P.M. (1 hr.)	72 + 108 = 180 km	124 km
6 to 7 P.M. (1 hr.)	180 + 108 = 288 km	124 + 124 = 248 km
7 to 8 P.M. (1 hr.)	288 + 108 = 396 km	248 + 124 = 372 km
8 to 9 P.M. (1 hr.)	396 + 108 = 504 km	372 + 124 = 496 km
9 to 9.30 P.M. (30 min.)	108 ÷ 2 = 54 km 504 + 54 = 558 km	124 ÷ 2 = 62 km 496 + 62 = 558 km

From 5 P.M. to 9:30 P.M., it was 4 hr. 30 min.
Claudia took **4 hr. 30 min.** to catch up with Kumiko.
(b) 600 – 558 = 42 km
They were **42 km** away from Beach Town when Claudia caught up with Kumiko.

Unit 8: Circles

1. **O**
2. **OA, OB, OC, OD, OF, OG**
3. **FB, GC**
4. (b) **semicircle**

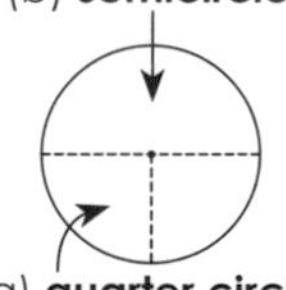

(a) **quarter circle**

5. **14, 44 in.**
Diameter = 14 in.
Circumference = $\pi d = \frac{22}{7} \times 14$ = 44 in.
6. **56, 176 cm**
Diameter = 56 cm
Circumference = $\pi d = \frac{22}{7} \times 56$ = 176 cm
7. **42, 132 ft.**
Diameter = 2 × 21 = 42 ft.
Circumference = $\pi d = \frac{22}{7} \times 42$ = 132 ft.
8. **5, 31.4 m**
Radius = 10 ÷ 2 = 5 m
Circumference = $2\pi r$ = 2 × 3.14 × 5 = 31.4 m
9. **7.5, 47.1 yd.**
Radius = 15 ÷ 2 = 7.5 yd.
Circumference = $2\pi r$ = 2 × 3.14 × 7.5 = 47.1 yd.
10. **48, 301.44 in.**
Radius = 48 in.
Circumference = $2\pi r$ = 2 × 3.14 × 48 = 301.44 in.
11. **66 cm**
Circumference of the semicircle
$= \frac{2\pi r}{2} = \pi r = \frac{22}{7} \times 14$ = 44 cm
Circumference of the quarter circle
$= \frac{2\pi r}{4} = \frac{1}{2}\pi r = \frac{1}{2} \times \frac{22}{7} \times 14$ = 22 cm
Perimeter of the figure = 44 + 22 = 66 cm
12. **203.94 cm**
Circumference of the semicircle
$= \frac{2\pi r}{2} = \pi r$ = 3.14 × 21 = 65.94 cm

Length of the rectangle with the semicircle
= 60 – 21 – 21
= 18 cm
Perimeter of the shaded part
= 30 + 60 + 30 + 18 + 65.94
= 203.94 cm

13. **113.37 in.**
Width of the shaded part = 14 – 10 = 4 in.
Length of the rectangle = 10 + 21 + 10 = 41 in.
Circumference of the semicircle
$= \frac{2\pi r}{2} = \pi r = 3.14 \times \frac{21}{2} = 32.97$ in.
Circumference of the quadrant
$= \frac{2\pi r}{4} = \frac{1}{2}\pi r = \frac{1}{2} \times 3.14 \times 10 = 15.7$ in.
Perimeter of the shaded part
= 4 + 41 + 4 + 15.7 + 32.97 + 15.7
= 113.37 in.

14. **252 cm**
Circumference of each semicircle
$= \frac{2\pi r}{2} = \pi r = \frac{22}{7} \times \frac{49}{2} = 77$ cm
Perimeter of the shaded part = 49 + 77 + 77 + 49
= 252 cm

15. **571 ft.**
Circumference of each semicircle
$= \frac{2\pi r}{2} = \pi r = 3.14 \times \frac{100}{2} = 157$ ft.
Perimeter of the figure = 157 + 157 + 157 + 100
= 571 ft.

16. **113.04 ft.²**
Area $= \pi r^2 = 3.14 \times 6 \times 6 = 113.04$ ft.²

17. **616 mi.²**
Area $= \pi r^2 = \frac{22}{7} \times 14 \times 14 = 616$ mi.²

18. **379.94 cm²**
Area $= \pi r^2 = 3.14 \times \frac{22}{2} \times \frac{22}{2} = 379.94$ cm²

19. **3,850 yd.²**
Area $= \pi r^2 = \frac{22}{7} \times \frac{70}{2} \times \frac{70}{2} = 3{,}850$ yd.²

20. **308 in.²**
Area $= \frac{\pi r^2}{2} = \frac{22}{7} \times \frac{28}{2} \times \frac{28}{2} \times \frac{1}{2} = 308$ in.²

21. **127.17 cm²**
Area $= \frac{\pi r^2}{2} = \frac{3.14 \times 9 \times 9}{2} = 127.17$ cm²

22. **154 m²**
Area $= \frac{\pi r^2}{4} = \frac{22}{7} \times 14 \times 14 \times \frac{1}{4} = 154$ m²

23. **12.56 in.²**
Area $= \frac{\pi r^2}{4} = \frac{3.14 \times 4 \times 4}{4} = 12.56$ in.²

24. **462 ft.²**
Area $= \frac{\pi r^2}{4} \times 3 = \frac{22}{7} \times 14 \times 14 \times \frac{1}{4} \times 3 = 462$ ft.²

25. **1039.5 cm²**
Radius = 42 ÷ 2 = 21 cm
Area $= \frac{\pi r^2}{4} \times 3 = \frac{22}{7} \times 21 \times 21 \times \frac{1}{4} \times 3 = 1039.5$ cm²

26. **536.94 cm²**
Diameter of each semicircle $= \frac{28 - 8}{2} = 10$ cm
Radius of each semicircle = 10 ÷ 2 = 5 cm
Area of each semicircle $= \frac{\pi r^2}{2} = \frac{3.14 \times 5 \times 5}{2} = 39.25$ cm²
Area of the circle $= \pi r^2 = 3.14 \times \frac{28}{2} \times \frac{28}{2} = 615.44$ cm²
Area of the shaded part = 615.44 – 39.25 – 39.25 = 536.94 cm²

27. **2,128 in.²**
Area of each circle $= \pi r^2 = \frac{22}{7} \times 21 \times 21$
= 1,386 in.²
Area of the square = 70 × 70 = 4,900 in.²
Area of the shaded part = 4,900 – 1,386 – 1,386
= 2,128 in.²

28. **593.46 cm²**
Area of the big circle $= \pi r^2$
= 3.14 × (10 + 7) × (10 + 7)
= 907.46 cm²
Area of the small circle $= \pi r^2 = 3.14 \times 10 \times 10$
= 314 cm²
Area of the shaded part = 907.46 – 314
= 539.46 cm²

29. **924 in.²**
Area of the semicircle $= \frac{\pi r^2}{2} = \frac{22}{7} \times \frac{56}{2} \times \frac{56}{2} \times \frac{1}{2}$
= 1,232 in.²
Area of each quadrant $= \frac{\pi r^2}{4} = \frac{22}{7} \times 14 \times 14 \times \frac{1}{4}$
= 154 in.²
Area of the shaded part = 1,232 – 154 – 154
= 924 in.²

30. **500.045 cm²**
Radius of the bigger circle = 35 ÷ 2 = 17.5 cm
Area of the bigger circle $= \pi r^2 = 3.14 \times 17.5 \times 17.5$
= 961.625 cm²
Area of each small circle $= \pi r^2 = 3.14 \times 7 \times 7$
= 153.86 cm²
Area of the shaded part = 961.625 – (3 × 153.86)
= 500.045 cm²

31. **62.8 in.**
Circumference $= 2\pi r = 2 \times 3.14 \times 10 = 62.8$ in.

32. **77.1 cm**
Radius of the semicircle = 30 ÷ 2 = 15 cm
Circumference of the semicircle $= \frac{2\pi r}{2} = \pi r$
= 3.14 × 15
= 47.1 cm
47.1 + 30 = 77.1 cm

33. **66 ft.**
Circumference $= \pi d = \frac{22}{7} \times 21 = 66$ ft.

34. **880 cm**
Circumference of a tire $= \pi d = \frac{22}{7} \times 70 = 220$ cm
4 × 220 = 880 cm

35. **706.5 in.²**
Radius = 60 ÷ 2 = 30 in.
Area of the circular piece of cloth $= \pi r^2$
= 3.14 × 30 × 30
= 2,826 in.²
2,826 ÷ 4 = 706.5 in.²

36. **3,118.5 cm²**
$\frac{\pi r^2}{4} = \frac{22}{7} \times 63 \times 63 \times \frac{1}{4} = 3{,}118.5$ cm

37. **126 in.²**
Area of the quadrant $= \frac{\pi r^2}{4} = \frac{22}{7} \times 21 \times 21 \times \frac{1}{4}$
= 346.5 in.²
Area of the triangle $= \frac{1}{2} \times W \times H = \frac{1}{2} \times 21 \times 21$
= 220.5 in.²
Area of the shaded part = 346.5 – 220.5 = 126 in.²

38. **289π cm²**
Radius = 34 ÷ 2 = 17 cm
$\pi r^2 = \pi \times 17 \times 17 = 289\pi$

39. **104.06 ft.²**
Radius of the semicircle = 22 ÷ 2 = 11 ft.
Area of each semicircle = $\frac{\pi r^2}{2} = \frac{3.14 \times 11 \times 11}{2}$
= 189.97 ft.²
Area of the square = 22 × 22 = 484 ft.²
Area of the shaded part = 484 – 189.97 – 189.97
= 104.06 ft.²

40. (a) Area of the rectangle = L × W = 100 × 70
= 7,000 yd.²
Area of each semicircle = $\frac{\pi r^2}{2} = \frac{22}{7} \times \frac{70}{2} \times \frac{70}{2} \times \frac{1}{2}$
= 1,925 yd.²
7,000 + 1,925 + 1,925 = 10,850 yd.²
The area of the field is **10,850 yd.²**.
(b) Circumference of each semicircle = $\frac{\pi d}{2} = \frac{22}{7} \times 70 \times \frac{1}{2}$
= 110 yd.
110 + 100 + 110 + 100 = 420 yd.
The perimeter of the field is 420 yd.
8 × 420 = 3,360 yd.
She runs **3,360 yd.**

41. Circumference of each large semicircle
$= \frac{\pi d}{2} = \frac{3.14 \times 18}{2}$ = 28.26 cm
Circumference of each small semicircle
$= \frac{\pi d}{2} = \frac{3.14 \times (18 \div 2)}{2}$ = 14.13 cm
14.13 + 28.26 + 14.13 + 28.26 + 14.13 + 9 + 9 = 116.91 cm
The length of the piece of wire needed to form this figure is **116.91 cm.**

42. Radius of each quadrant = 42 ÷ 2 = 21 in.
Area of each quadrant = $\frac{\pi r^2}{4} = \frac{22}{7} \times 21 \times 21 \times \frac{1}{4}$ = 346.5 in.²
Area of a quarter of the square = $\frac{1}{4} \times 42 \times 42$ = 441 in.²
Area of each unshaded area in a quarter-square
= 441 – 346.5
= 94.5 in.²
Area of the shaded area in a quarter of the square
= 441 – 94.5 – 94.5
= 252 in.²
4 × 252 = 1,008 in.²
The area of the shaded portion in the figure is **1,008 in.²**.

43. Radius of each quadrant = 60 ÷ 2 = 30 cm
Circumference of each quadrant = $\frac{2\pi r}{4}$
$= \frac{2 \times 3.14 \times 30}{4}$
= 47.1 cm
4 × 47.1 = 188.4 cm
The perimeter of the shaded part is **188.4 cm**.

44. Area of the triangle = $\frac{1}{2} \times W \times H = \frac{1}{2} \times 12 \times 16$
= 96 ft.²
Area of the bigger semicircle
$= \frac{\pi r^2}{2} = \frac{22}{7} \times \frac{20}{2} \times \frac{20}{2} \times \frac{1}{2} = 157\frac{1}{7}$ ft.²
Area of the smaller semicircle
$= \frac{\pi r^2}{2} = \frac{22}{7} \times \frac{16}{2} \times \frac{16}{2} \times \frac{1}{2} = 100\frac{4}{7}$ ft.²
$96 + 157\frac{1}{7} + 100\frac{4}{7} = 353\frac{5}{7}$ ft.²
The area of the figure is **$353\frac{5}{7}$ ft.²**.

Review 1

1. **(4)**
Distance = Rate × Time = $18 \times \frac{10}{60}$ = 3 km
Time = Distance ÷ Rate = 3 ÷ 4 = $\frac{3}{4}$ hr. = 45 min.

2. **(3)**
Average rate of speed = Total distance ÷ Total time
= (865 + 719) ÷ (18 + 30)
= 1584 ÷ 48
= 33 ft./min.

3. **(2)**
From 6:00 P.M. to 2:00 A.M., it was 8 hours.
Rate = Distance ÷ Time
= 160 ÷ 8
= 20 mph

4. **(3)**
$2\pi r = 2 \times \pi \times 8 = 16\pi$

5. **(3)**
Circumference of the semicircles = $2 \times \frac{2\pi r}{2} = 2\pi r$
$= 2 \times 3.14 \times \frac{150}{2}$
= 471 yd.
150 + 150 + 471 = 771 yd.

6. **(2)**
Average rate of speed = Total distance ÷ Total time
= (2 × 21) ÷ ($1\frac{1}{2}$ + 2)
= 12 mph

7. **(3)**
Radius of the circle = 12 ÷ 2 = 6 cm
Circumference of each quadrant = $\frac{2\pi r}{4} = \frac{2 \times 3.14 \times 6}{4}$
= 9.42 cm
Circumference of the figure = 6 + 6 + 9.42 + 6 + 9.42 + 6
= 42.84 cm

8. **918.75π in.²**
Area of the large semicircle = $\frac{1}{2} \times \pi r^2 = \frac{1}{2} \times \pi \times \frac{70}{2} \times \frac{70}{2}$
= 612.5π in.²
Area of the two small semicircles
$= 2 \times \frac{1}{2} \times \pi r^2 = \pi r^2 = \pi \times \frac{35}{2} \times \frac{35}{2} = 306.25\pi$ in.²
$612.5\pi + 306.25\pi = 918.75\pi$ in.²

9. **50 min.**
$\frac{60}{100} \times 8$ = 4.8 km
Rate = Distance ÷ Time = 4.8 ÷ 30 = 0.16 km/min.
Time = Distance ÷ Rate = 8 ÷ 0.16 = 50 min.

10. **50 min.**
Distance = Rate × Time = $45 \times \frac{42}{60}$ = 31.5 mi.
100% → 45 mph
100% – 16% → $\frac{45}{100} \times 84$ = 37.8 mph
Time = Distance ÷ Rate = 31.5 ÷ 37.8
= 0.83 hr. = 50 min.

11. **174 in.**
Circumference of the semicircle = $\frac{\pi d}{2} = \frac{22}{7} \times 42 \times \frac{1}{2}$
= 66 in.
Circumference of the quadrant = $\frac{2\pi r}{4} = 2 \times \frac{22}{7} \times 42 \times \frac{1}{4}$
= 66 in.
66 + 66 + 42 = 174 in.

12. **30.96 cm²**
Edge of the square = $\sqrt{144}$ = 12 cm
Area of the quadrant = $\frac{1}{4} \times \pi r^2 = \frac{1}{4} \times 3.14 \times 12 \times 12$
= 113.04 cm²

144 – 113.04 = 30.96 cm^2

13. **231 ft.²**
Area of the big semicircle = $\frac{1}{2} \times \pi r^2 = \frac{1}{2} \times \frac{22}{7} \times 14 \times 14$
= 308 ft.²
Area of the small semicircle = $\frac{1}{2} \times \pi r^2 = \frac{1}{2} \times \frac{22}{7} \times \frac{14}{2} \times \frac{14}{2}$
= 77 ft.²
308 – 77 = 231 ft.²

14. **$3\frac{1}{2}$ hr.**
Time = Distance ÷ Rate = 105 ÷ 50 = $2\frac{1}{10}$ hr.
$\frac{3}{4} \rightarrow$ 105 km
$\frac{1}{4} \rightarrow$ 105 ÷ 3 = 35 km
Time = Distance ÷ Rate = 35 ÷ 25 = $1\frac{2}{5}$ hr.
$2\frac{1}{10} + 1\frac{2}{5} = 3\frac{1}{2}$ hr.

15. **95.97 in.**
Circumference of the quadrant = $\frac{2\pi r}{4} = \frac{2 \times 3.14 \times 21}{4}$
= 32.97 in.
21 + 21 + 21 + 32.97 = 95.97 in.

16. Distance = Rate × Time = 28 × $\frac{15}{60}$ = 7 mi.
The distance between Peter's house and the beach is 7 mi.
Time = Distance ÷ Rate = 7 ÷ 35 = $\frac{1}{5}$ hr. or 12 min.
Anna will take **12 min.** to drive the same distance.

17. Area of the rectangle = 30 × 20 = 600 in.²
Area of the semicircle = $\frac{1}{2} \times \pi r^2 = \frac{1}{2} \times 3.14 \times 10 \times 10$
= 157 in.²
Area of the quadrant = $\frac{1}{4} \times \pi r^2 = \frac{1}{4} \times 3.14 \times 10 \times 10$
= 78.5 in.²
600 – 157 – 78.5 = 364.5 in.²
The area of the shaded part is **364.5 in.²**.

18. Area of the rectangle = (2 × 28) × 28 = 1,568 in.²
Area of each quadrant = $\frac{1}{4} \times \pi r^2 = \frac{1}{4} \times \frac{22}{7} \times 28 \times 28$
= 616 in.²
1,568 – 616 – 616 = 336 in.²
The area of the shaded part is **336 in.²**.

19. (a) Length of the square = 4 × 5 = 20 cm
Area of the square = 20 × 20 = 400 cm²
Area of the semicircle = $\frac{1}{2} \times \pi r^2 = \frac{1}{2} \times 3.14 \times \frac{5}{2} \times \frac{5}{2}$
= 9.8125 cm²
Area of each quadrant = $\frac{1}{4} \times \pi r^2$
= $\frac{1}{4} \times 3.14 \times 5 \times 5$
= 19.625 cm²
400 – 9.8125 – (3 × 19.625) = 331.3125 ≈ 331 cm²
The area of the shaded part is **331 cm²**.
(b) Circumference of each quadrant
= $\frac{2\pi r}{4} = \frac{2 \times 3.14 \times 5}{4}$ = 7.85 cm
Circumference of the semicircle
= $\frac{\pi d}{2} = \frac{3.14 \times 5}{2}$ = 7.85 cm
7.85 + 10 + 7.85 + 10 + 7.85 + 10 + 7.85 + 15 = 76.4 ≈ 76 cm
The perimeter of the shaded part is **76 cm**.

20. (a) Time = Distance ÷ Rate = 360 ÷ 80 = $4\frac{1}{2}$ hr.
$4\frac{1}{2}$ hr. after 10:00 A.M. was 2:30 P.M.
Vanessa left the house at 12:00.
Therefore, she took $2\frac{1}{2}$ hr. to travel 360 km.
Rate = Distance ÷ Time = 360 ÷ $2\frac{1}{2}$ = 144 km/h
Vanessa's speed was **144 km/h**.
(b) From 10:00 A.M. to 3:30 P.M., it was $5\frac{1}{2}$ hr.
Distance = Rate × Time = 80 × $5\frac{1}{2}$ = 440 km
Travis traveled 440 km at 3:30 P.M.
From 12:00 to 3:30 P.M., it was $3\frac{1}{2}$ hr.
Distance = Rate × Time = 144 × $3\frac{1}{2}$ = 504 km
Vanessa traveled 504 km at 3:30 P.M.
504 – 440 = 64 km
They would be **64 km** apart at 3:30 P.M.

Unit 9: Pie Charts

1. (a) **160 students**
2 × 80 = 160
(b) **320 students**
4 × 80 = 320
(c) **48 students**
$\frac{3}{20}$ × 320 = 48
(d) $\mathbf{\frac{1}{2}}$

2. (a) **17%**
100% – 45% – 12% – 26% = 17%
(b) **2,800 tourists**
17% → 476
1% → 476 ÷ 17 = 28
100% → 28 × 100 = 2,800
(c) **392 more Canadian tourists**
26% – 12% = 14%
$\frac{14}{100}$ × 2,800 = 392
(d) **1,512 Indian tourists**
$\frac{45}{100}$ × 2,800 = 1,260
100% → 1,260
1% → 1,260 ÷ 100 = 12.6
120% → 12.6 × 120 = 1,512

3. (a) **120 families**
$\frac{1}{3}$ × 360 = 120
(b) **150 families**
360 ÷ 4 = 90
There are 90 families with 1 child.
360 – 90 – 120 = 150
(c) **120 families**
4 + 1 = 5 units → 150
1 unit → 150 ÷ 5 = 30
4 units → 4 × 30 = 120
(d) **420 children**
(90 × 1) + (120 × 2) + (30 × 3) = 420

4. (a) **200 students**
$\frac{2}{5} \rightarrow$ 20
$\frac{1}{5} \rightarrow$ 20 ÷ 2 = 10
$\frac{5}{5}$ = 5 × 10 = 50
50 students liked bowling.
4 × 50 = 200
(b) **30%**
$\frac{90}{360}$ × 100% = 25%
25% of the students liked bowling.

$100\% - 5\% - 40\% - 25\% = 30\%$

(c) **70 students**

$40\% - 5\% = 35\%$

$\frac{35}{100} \times 200 = 70$

(d) **50 girls**

$\frac{5}{100} \times 200 = 10$

$10 \div 2 = 5$ girls

$10\% \rightarrow 5$ girls

$100\% \rightarrow 10 \times 5 = 50$ girls

5. (a) **126 Rocky Road and vanilla ice-cream cones**

Rocky Road:chocolate chip:vanilla

14 × (2:4 → 28:56) ×14 :7 → :98) ×14

$28 + 98 = 126$

(b) **98 strawberry and chocolate ice-cream cones**

$100\% - 15\% - 20\% = 65\%$

$65\% \rightarrow 28 + 56 + 98 = 182$

$35\% \rightarrow \frac{182}{65} \times 35 = 98$

(c) **chocolate, chocolate chip**

$\frac{182}{65} \times 20 = 56$ chocolate ice-cream cones

(d) **280 ice-cream cones**

$65\% \rightarrow 182$

$100\% \rightarrow \frac{182}{65} \times 100 = 280$

6. (a) **$945**

$\frac{75}{100} \times \$540 = \$405$

$\$540 + \$405 = \$945$

(b) **$210**

$1 - \frac{1}{3} - \frac{1}{18} - \frac{1}{2} = \frac{1}{9}$

$1 = 2 \times \$945 = \$1,890$

$\frac{1}{9} \times \$1,890 = \$210$

(c) **$7,560**

$\frac{1}{3} \times \$1,890 = \$630$

$12 \times \$630 = \$7,560$

(d) **$1,575**

$120\% \rightarrow \$1,890$

$1\% \rightarrow \$1,890 \div 120 = \$15.75$

$100\% \rightarrow 100\% \times \$15.75 = \$1,575$

7. (a) **750 mathematics assessment books**

$80\% \rightarrow 480 + 120 = 600$

$100\% \rightarrow \frac{600}{80} \times 100 = 750$

(b) **330 more English assessment books**

$750 - 480 - 120 = 150$ Social Studies assessment books

$480 - 150 = 330$

(c) **870 science and mathematics assessment books**

$120 + 750 = 870$

(d) **32%**

$2 \times 750 = 1500$

$\frac{480}{1500} \times 100 = 32\%$

8. (a) **2,100 tourists**

$\frac{4}{5} \rightarrow 420$

$\frac{5}{5} \rightarrow \frac{420}{4} \times 5 = 525$

$4 \times 525 = 2,100$

(b) **210 more tourists**

$\frac{15}{100} \times 2,100 = 315$

315 tourists went to the art museum.

$525 - 315 = 210$

(c) **840 tourists**

$420 + 525 + 315 = 1,260$

$2,100 - 1,260 = 840$

(d) **40%**

$\frac{840}{2,100} \times 100 = 40\%$

9. (a) **12%**

$100\% - 40\% = 60\%$

$\frac{1}{5} \times 60\% = 12\%$

(b) **4,500 fiction books**

$1 - \frac{1}{5} = \frac{4}{5}$ of fiction books are English

$\frac{4}{5} - \frac{1}{5} \rightarrow 2,700$

$\frac{3}{5} \rightarrow 2,700$

$\frac{1}{5} \rightarrow 2,700 \div 3 = 900$

$900 \times 5 = 4,500$

(c) **7,500 fiction and non-fiction books**

$100\% - 40\% = 60\%$

$60\% \rightarrow 4,500$

$1\% \rightarrow 4,500 \div 60 = 75$

$100\% \rightarrow 100 \times 75 = 7,500$

(d) **3:50**

$\frac{40}{100} \times 7,500 = 3,000$ non-fiction books

$\frac{15}{100} \times 3,000 = 450$ non-English non-fiction books

non-English non-fiction:total books

450:7500

3:50

10. (a) **$1,440**

Judy:Trina

120 × (7:12 → 840:1,440) × 120

(b) **$960**

$\frac{2}{9} \times \$4,320 = \$960$

(c) **$120**

$\$4,320 - \$840 - \$1,440 - \$960 = \$1,080$

$\$1,080 - \$960 = \$120$

(d) **2:3:9**

Anna:Trina:Total sum

960:1440:4320

2:3:9

Unit 10: Area and Perimeter

1. (a) Area of rectangle 1 = $18 \times 7 = 126$ cm^2

Area of rectangle 2 = $21 \times 7 = 147$ cm^2

Area of the figure = $126 + 147 =$ **273 cm^2**

(b) Perimeter of the figure

$= 18 + 7 + 18 + 7 + 7 + 21 + 7 + 7$

= **92 cm**

2. Area of the equilateral triangle = $\frac{1}{2} \times 28 \times 20 = 280$ in.^{2}

Area of the semicircle = $\frac{\pi r^2}{2} = \frac{22}{7} \times \frac{14}{2} \times \frac{14}{2} \times \frac{1}{2} = 77$ in.^{2}

Area of the shaded part = $280 - 77 =$ **203 in.^{2}**

3. (a) Area of the rectangle = $12 \times 10 = 120$ cm^2

Area of each triangle = $\frac{1}{2} \times 8 \times 8 = 32$ cm^2

Area of the shaded part = $120 - 32 - 32 =$ **56 cm^2**

(b) Perimeter of the shaded part = $4 + 2 + 11 + 4 + 2 + 11$

= **34 cm**

4. Area of the square = $14 \times 14 = 196$ ft.^{2}
Area of the quadrant = $\frac{\pi r^2}{4} = \frac{22}{7} \times 14 \times 14 \times \frac{1}{4} = 154$ ft.^{2}
Area of the shaded portion = 196 – 154 = **42 ft.^{2}**

5. Area of the rectangle = $20 \times 8 = 160$ cm^2
Area of each triangle = $\frac{1}{2} \times 8 \times 8 = 32$ cm^2
Area of the shaded part = 160 – 32 – 32 = **96 cm^2**

6. Area of the square = $15 \times 15 = 225$ yd.^{2}
Area of big triangle = $\frac{1}{2} \times 15 \times 15 = 112.5$ yd.^{2}
Area of small triangle = $\frac{1}{2} \times 5 \times 13 = 32.5$ yd.^{2}
Area of the shaded part = 225 – 112.5 – 32.5 = **80 yd.^{2}**

7. Area of the rectangle = $10 \times 8 = 80$ cm^2
Area of the triangle = $\frac{1}{2} \times 10 \times 9 = 45$ cm^2
Area of the the trapezoid = 80 + 45 = **125 cm^2**

8. (a) Perimeter of the figure = 7 + 18 + 4 + 4 + 7 + 18
= **58 in.**
(b) Area of each big rectangle = $7 \times 6 = 42$ in.^{2}
Area of small rectangle = $6 \times 3 = 18$ in.^{2}
Area of the figure = 42 + 18 + 42 = **102 in.^{2}**

9. Area of each triangle = $\frac{1}{2} \times 10 \times 10 = 50$ cm^2
Area of the shaded parts = 3×50 = **150 cm^2**

10. Area of the rectangle = $70 \times 20 = 1{,}400$ cm^2
Area of the each circle = $\pi r^2 = 3.14 \times \frac{10}{2} \times \frac{10}{2}$
= 78.5 cm^2
Area of the shaded portion = 1,400 – (14 × 78.5)
= **301 cm^2**

Review 2

1. **(3)**
Books = $\frac{1}{6} \times \$192 = \$32$
Stamps = $\frac{1}{12} \times \$192 = \$16$
$32 + $16 = $48

2. **(4)**
$1 - \frac{1}{12} - \frac{1}{24} - \frac{1}{6} = \frac{17}{24}$
$\frac{17}{24} \times \$192 = \$136$

3. **(1)**
$\frac{1}{24} \times \$192 = \$8$

4. **(2)**
Area of the triangle = $\frac{1}{2} \times 10 \times (11 - 6) = 25$ cm^2
Area of the trapezoid = $(10 \times 6) + \left(\frac{1}{2} \times 3 \times 6\right) = 69$ cm^2
25 + 69 = 94 cm^2

5. **(3)**
Area of big triangle = $\frac{1}{2} \times 15 \times 24 = 180$ in.^{2}
Area of small triangle = $\frac{1}{2} \times 24 \times 9 = 108$ in.^{2}
180 + 108 = 288 in.^{2}

6. **(3)**
Circumference of the semicircle = $\frac{\pi d}{2} = \frac{3.14 \times 20}{2}$
= 31.4 cm
20 + 20 + 20 + 31.4 = 91.4 cm

7. **(2)**
Area of the rectangle = $84 \times 42 = 3528$ cm^2
Area of the circle = $\pi r^2 = \frac{22}{7} \times \frac{42}{2} \times \frac{42}{2} = 1386$ cm^2
3,528 – 1,386 = 2,142 cm^2

8. **524 in.^{2}**
Area of the rectangular cardboard = 38×30
= 1140 in.^{2}
Area of the circle = $\pi r^2 = \frac{22}{7} \times 14 \times 14 = 616$ in.^{2}
1,140 – 616 = 524 in.^{2}

9. **125 cm^2**
Area of each triangle = $\frac{1}{2} \times 10 \times 5 = 25$ cm^2
$5 \times 25 = 125$ cm^2

10. **40 students**
30% → 12
10% → 12 ÷ 3 = 4
100% → 10 × 4 = 40

11. **10 students**
$\frac{25}{100} \times 40 = 10$

12. **8 students**
100% – 25% – 15% – 30% = 30%
20% of the students like reading.
$\frac{20}{100} \times 40 = 8$

13. **66 cm**
2 + 17 + 2 + 5 + 5 + 9 + 7 + 9 + 5 + 5 = 66 cm

14. **207 ft.^{2}**
Area of the rectangle = $18 \times 9 = 162$ ft.^{2}
Area of the triangle = $\frac{1}{2} \times 9 \times 10 = 45$ ft.^{2}
162 + 45 = 207 ft.^{2}

15. **117.5 cm^2**
Area of the square tray = $14 \times 14 = 196$ cm^2
Area of each circle = $\pi r^2 = 3.14 \times \frac{5}{2} \times \frac{5}{2} = 19.625$ cm^2
196 – (4 × 19.625) = 117.5 cm^2

16. 100% – 20% – 25% – 25% = 30%
$\frac{30}{100} \times 300 = 90$
He sold **90** watermelons.

17. $\frac{25}{100} \times 300 = 75$
He sold 75 cantaloupe.
$\frac{20}{100} \times 300 = 60$
He sold 60 mangoes.
(75 × $1.30) + (60 × $1.60) = $193.50
He would make **$193.50**.

18. Area of the puzzle = $120 \times 60 = 7{,}200$ cm^2
Area of missing piece = $(4 \times 4) + (2 \times 1) + \left(\frac{3.14 \times 1 \times 1}{2}\right)$
= 19.57 cm^2
7,200 – 19.57 = 7,180.43 cm^2
The area of the remaining puzzle is **7,180.43 cm^2**.

19. 40 – 4 – 32 = 4 in.
The two triangles are identical.
Area of the triangles = $2 \times \frac{1}{2} \times 4 \times 18 = 72$ in.^{2}
Area of the rectangle = $32 \times 18 = 576$ in.^{2}
72 + 576 = 648 in.^{2}
The area of the display sign is **648 in.^{2}**

20. 42 – 14 – 14 = 14 cm
The width of the rectangle is 14 cm.
Circumference of each semicircle = $\pi d = \frac{22}{7} \times 14$
= 44 cm
44 + 44 + 44 + 14 + 44 + 44 + 44 + 14 = 292 cm
The perimeter of the figure is **292 cm**.

Unit 11: Volume

1. **23**
2. **35**
3. **18**
4. **44**
5. **48**
6. **8**
7. **9**
8. **12**
9. **19**
10. **14**
11. **990 in.³**
    Volume = 9 × 5 × 22 = 990 in.³
12. **3,128 cm³**
    Volume = 23 × 17 × 8 = 3,128 cm³
13. **8000 in.³**
    Volume = 20 × 20 × 20 = 8,000 in.³
14. **13 cm**
    130 cm³ = 5 × 2 × H
    $H = \frac{130}{2 \times 5} = 13$ cm
15. **5 cm**
    480 cm³ = 12 × B × 8
    $W = \frac{480}{12 \times 8} = 5$ cm
16. **8 in.**
    224 in.³ = L × 4 × 7
    $L = \frac{224}{4 \times 7} = 8$ in.
17. **5,184 cm³**
    Volume of the cube = 12 × 12 × 12 = 1,728 cm³
    Volume of the rectangular block = 12 × 12 × 24 = 3,456 cm³
    Volume of the solid = 1,728 + 3,456 = 5,148 cm³
18. **13 in.**
    Length of each edge = $\sqrt[3]{2,197}$ = 13 in.
19. **24 cm**
    Height = $\frac{4,224}{176}$ = 24 cm
20. **520 cm³**
    Volume of the solid = 30 × 13 × 8 = 3,120 cm³
    Volume of the rectangular block = 25 × 13 × 8
    = 2,600 cm³
    Volume of the remaining solid = 3,120 – 2,600
    = 520 cm³
21. **512 in.³**
    Volume of 16 cubes = 16 × 4 × 4 × 4 = 1,024 in.³
    Volume of the remaining 8 cubes = 1,024 ÷ 2
    = 512 in.³
22. **1,664 cm³**
    Volume of the rectangular prism = 32 × 28 × 4 = 3,584 cm³
    Volume of the hole that was cut = 24 × 20 × 4
    = 1,920 cm³
    Volume of the frame = 3,584 – 1,920 = 1,664 cm³
23. **36.3 L**
    Volume of water = $\frac{3}{4}$ × 55 × 22 × 40 = 36,300 cm³
    = 36.3 L
24. **7 L 200 mL**
    Volume of water needed to fill the vase to its brim
    = $\frac{4}{5}$ × 15 × 12 × 50 = 7,200 cm³
    = 7 L 200 mL
25. **24 cm**
    Volume of water = 36 × 26 × H
    11,232 = 36 × 26 × H
    $H = \frac{11,232}{36 \times 26} = 12$ cm
    Height of the tank = 2 × 12 = 24 cm
26. **240 min.**
    Volume of water in the tank = 100 × 330 × 80
    = 2,640,000 cm³
    = 2,640 L
    2,640 ÷ 11 = 240 min.
27. **45 cm**
    Height = 24,300 ÷ 1,350 = 18 cm
    $\frac{2}{5} \rightarrow$ 18 cm
    $\frac{1}{5} \rightarrow$ 18 ÷ 2 = 9 cm
    9 × 5 = 45 cm
28. **4 in.**
    Volume of each cube = 576 ÷ 9 = 64 in.³
    Edge of each cube = $\sqrt[3]{64}$ = 4 in.
29. **40 cm**
    $\frac{3}{4} \rightarrow$ 63 L
    $\frac{1}{4} \rightarrow$ 63 ÷ 3 = 21 L
    Volume of the fish tank = 4 × 21 = 84 L
    = 84,000 cm³
    Height = $\frac{84,000}{35 \times 60}$ = 40 cm
30. **18 cm**
    Volume of a 12-cm cube = 12 × 12 × 12
    = 1,728 cm³
    Height of the rectangular solid = $\frac{1,728}{16 \times 6}$ = 18 cm
31. **361 cm²**
    Edge of a cubical tank = $\sqrt[3]{6,859}$ = 19 cm
    Base area of the cubical tank = 19 × 19 = 361 cm²
32. **125 cm²**
    1.65 L = 1.65 × 1,000 = 1,650 cm³
    $\frac{3}{5} \rightarrow$ 1,650 cm³
    $\frac{1}{5} \rightarrow$ 1,650 ÷ 3 = 550 cm³
    5 × 550 = 2,750 cm³
    The tank can hold 2,750 cm³ of water when it is full.
    Area of its base = 2,750 ÷ 22 = 125 cm²
33. **13 cm**
    Volume of water = $\frac{3}{4}$ × 35 × 22 × 38 = 21,945 cm³
    11.935 L × 1,000 = 11,935 cm³
    21,945 – 11,935 = 10,010 cm³
    Height = $\frac{10,010}{35 \times 22}$ = 13 cm
34. **14 min.**
    Volume of container when it is completely filled with water = 56 × 50 × 60 = 168,000 cm³ = 168 L
    168 L ÷ 12 L = 14 min.
35. (a) 40 × 45 × 55 = 99,000 cm³ = 99 L
    The capacity of the container is **99 L.**
    (b) 99 ÷ 11 = 9 min.
    It will take **9 minutes** to drain all the water out of the container.
36. Volume of the rectangular prism = 20 × 24 × 40 = 19,200 in.³
    Volume of each cube = 19,200 ÷ 300 = 64 in.³
    $\sqrt[3]{64}$ = 4 in.
    The edge of each cube is **4 in.**
37. Volume of the cuboid = 24 × 14 × 27 = 9,072 cm³
    Volume of the hole = 20 × 10 × 27 = 5,400 cm³
    Volume of the remaining cuboid = 9,072 – 5,400
    = 3,672 cm³
    The volume of the remaining cuboid is **3,672 cm³.**

38. Volume of water in the rectangular tank
$= 16 \times 15 \times 20 = 4{,}800 \text{ in.}^3$
Height of water in the cubical tank $= \dfrac{4{,}800}{20 \times 20}$
$= 12$ in.
The height of the water in the cubical tank is **12 in.**

39. 1 m = 100 cm
Volume of the water tank $= 80 \times 60 \times 100$
$= 480{,}000 \text{ cm}^3$
$4.8 \text{ L} = 4{,}800 \text{ cm}^3$
Time needed to fill the water tank completely
$= 480{,}000 \div 4{,}800 = 100$ min.
It will take **100 minutes** to fill the water tank completely.

40. Volume of water collected for 1st 30 min.
$= 30 \times 32$
$= 960$ L
Volume of water collected for $2\frac{1}{2}$ hours
$= (150 \times 32) + (150 \times 40)$
$= 10{,}800$ L
Total volume of water collected $= 960 + 10{,}800$
$= 11{,}760$ L
Height of the water in the aquarium $= \dfrac{11{,}760{,}000}{320 \times 150}$
$= 245$ cm
The height of the water in it was **245 cm**.

Unit 12: Challenging Word Problems

1. Distance for the first $1\frac{1}{2}$ hr. $= R \times T = 33 \times 1\frac{1}{2}$
$= 49.5$ mi.
Distance for the next $1\frac{3}{4}$ hr. $= R \times T = 66 \times 1\frac{3}{4}$
$= 115.5$ mi.
Distance for the remaining $\frac{1}{2}$ hr. $= R \times T = 60 \times \frac{1}{2}$
$= 30$ mi.
Total distance $= 49.5 + 115.5 + 30 = 195$ mi.
Rate $=$ Distance $\div$ Time
$= 195 \div (1\frac{1}{2} + 1\frac{3}{4} + \frac{1}{2})$
$= 195 \div 3\frac{3}{4}$ hr.
$= 52$ mph
David's average rate of speed for the whole trip was **52 mph**.

2. 60
J | J | J | J | J | J | J | J | J | W | W | W | W | A | A | A | A | A | A | A | A
5 units → 60
1 unit → $60 \div 5 = 12$
$21 \times 12 = 252$
There were 252 raffle tickets.
$252 \times \$5 = \$1{,}260$
They collected **$1,260** altogether.

3. $(1 \times 1¢) + (3x \times 10¢) + (15 \times 25¢) = 406¢$
A set of 1 penny, 3 dimes, and 15 quarters is 406¢.
$6{,}496 \div 406 = 16$
$16 \times 3 = 48$
She had **48** dimes.

4. From 6:15 P.M. to 9:45 P.M., it was $3\frac{1}{2}$ hr.
$R \times T = 55 \times 3\frac{1}{2}$ hr. $= 192.5$ mi.
The distance between Town A and Town B was 192.5 mi.
$192.5 \div 62 = 3\frac{1}{10}$ hr. = 3 hr. 6 min.
The motorcyclist took 3 hr. 6 min. to reach Town B.
3 hr. 6 min. before 9:45 P.M. was 6:39 P.M.
The motorcyclist passed Town A at **6:39 P.M.**

5. (a) From 11 A.M. to 1:20 P.M., it was $2\frac{1}{3}$ hr.
$R = D \div T = 560 \div 2\frac{1}{3} = 240$ km/h
The rate of speed of both van and bus is 240 km/h.
$240 - 60 = 180$ km/h
$180 \div 2 = 90$ km/h
The average rate of speed of the bus is 90 km/h.
$90 + 60 = 150$ km/h
The van's average rate of speed is **150 km/h**.
(b) $D = R \times T = 90 \times 2\frac{1}{3} = 210$ km
The bus has traveled 210 km when it passes the van.
$560 - 210 = 350$ km
The bus is **350 km** away from Town X when it passes the van.

6. (a) 100% + 8% → $1,377
$100\% \rightarrow \dfrac{\$1{,}377}{108} \times 100 = \$1{,}275$
$\$1275 - \$150 = \$1125$
Kenny bought the laptop for $1,125.
100% + 25% → $1,125
$100\% \rightarrow \dfrac{\$1{,}125}{125} \times 100 = \$900$
Sanjiv bought the laptop at **$900**.
(b) 100% – 25% → $900
$100\% \rightarrow \dfrac{\$900}{75} \times 100 = \$1{,}200$
The original price of the laptop was **$1,200**.

7. 16 jeans + 20 T-shirts $= 4 \times \$129.10 = \$516.40$
25 jeans + 20 T-shirts $= 5 \times \$139.10 = \$695.50$
9 jeans $= \$695.50 - \$516.40 = \$179.10$
1 jeans $= \$179.10 \div 9 = \$19.90$
5 T-shirts $= \$129.10 - (4 \times \$19.90) = \$49.50$
1 T-shirt $= \$49.50 \div 5 = \$9.90$
$\$19.90 + \$9.90 = \$29.80$
The cost of a pair of jeans and T-shirt is **$29.80**.

8. 16 units – 8 units → 220 – 44
8 units → 176
1 unit → $176 \div 8 = 22$
She gave the seeds to **22** friends.

9. Before giving away some pens and pencils,
pens:pencils:erasers
$7 \times$ (6:13 → 42:91) $\times 7$:4 → :28) $\times 7$
After giving away some pens and pencils,
pens:pencils:erasers
$4 \times$ (4:17 → 16:68) $\times 4$:7 → :28) $\times 4$
$(42 + 91) - (16 + 68) = 49$
She gave away **49** pens and pencils.

10. chocolate:lollipops
5:2
5 + 2 units → $127.40
1 unit → $\$127.40 \div 7 = \$18.20$
$5 \times \$18.20 = \$91$
All chocolate cost $91.
$2 \times \$18.20 = \$36.40$
All lollipops cost $36.40.
chocolate:lollipops
7:4
$\$91 \div 7 = \$13$
Each unit of chocolate is $13.
$\$36.40 \div 4 = \$9.10$
Each unit of lollipops is $9.10.
$\$13 - \$9.10 = \$3.90$
The price difference between each unit of chocolate and lollipops is $3.90.

$\$3.90 \div \$0.15 = 26$
There is a difference of 26 between each unit of chocolate and lollipops.
$26 \times 4 = 104$
She bought **104** lollipops.

Review 3

1. **(1)**
$\frac{1}{4} \times 40 = 10$

2. **(1)**
$40 - 10 - 14 = 16$
16 students want to visit Europe.
$16 - 14 = 2$
2 more students want to visit Europe than the United States.

3. **(3)**
$\pi r^2 = 3.14 \times \frac{30}{2} \times \frac{30}{2} = 706.5 \text{ cm}^2$

4. **(1)**
$\frac{5}{7} \rightarrow 10{,}880 \text{ in.}^3$
$\frac{1}{7} \rightarrow 10{,}880 \div 5 = 2{,}176 \text{ in.}^3$
$7 \times 2{,}176 = 15{,}232 \text{ in.}^3$
Height $= \frac{15{,}232}{32 \times 28} = 17$ in.

5. **(1)**
Area of quadrant $= \frac{1}{4} \times \pi r^2 = \frac{1}{4} \times \frac{22}{7} \times 14 \times 14$
$= 154 \text{ in.}^2$
Area of semicircle $= \frac{1}{2} \times \pi r^2 = \frac{1}{2} \times \frac{22}{7} \times \frac{14}{2} \times \frac{14}{2}$
$= 77 \text{ in.}^2$
Area of the shaded part $= 154 - 77 = 77 \text{ in.}^2$

6. **(2)**
Volume of water in the tank $= 6 \times 5{,}000 = 30{,}000 \text{ cm}^3$
Height of water level $= 30{,}000 \div 480 = 62.5$ cm

7. **(1)**
Length of the square $= \sqrt{64} = 8$ cm
$30 + 8 + 8 + 8 + 8 + 30 + 16 = 108$ cm

8. **2,268 in.³**
$\frac{1}{5} \times 21 \times 18 \times 20 = 1{,}512 \text{ in.}^3$
$\frac{1}{2} \times 21 \times 18 \times 20 = 3{,}780 \text{ in.}^3$
$3{,}780 - 1{,}512 = 2{,}268 \text{ in.}^3$

9. **44 in.**
$\frac{\pi d}{4} = \frac{22}{7} \times 56 \times \frac{1}{4} = 44$ in.

10. $\mathbf{\frac{5}{36}}$
Boys who like green $= \frac{1}{4} = \frac{9}{36}$
Boys who like blue $= \frac{1}{9} = \frac{4}{36}$
Boys who like yellow $= \frac{18}{36}$
Girls $= 1 - \frac{9}{36} - \frac{4}{36} - \frac{18}{36} = \frac{5}{36}$

11. **20 in.**
Area of triangle $= \frac{1}{2} \times 5 \times 10 = 25 \text{ in.}^2$
Length of square $= \sqrt{25} = 5$ in.
Perimeter of square $= 4 \times 5 = 20$ in.

12. **23 min.**
Capacity of tank $= 46 \times 40 \times 20 = 36{,}800 \text{ cm}^3$
$36{,}800 \div 1{,}600 = 23$ min.

13. **73.5 in.²**
Area of the unshaded square $= 3.5 \times 3.5 = 12.25 \text{ in.}^2$
Area of the shaded region $= 6 \times 12.25 = 73.5 \text{ in.}^2$

14. **10 cm**
Height $= \frac{3{,}000}{300} = 10$ cm

15. **231.07 cm²**
Area of the rectangle $= 14 \times 22 = 308 \text{ cm}^2$
Area of the semicircle $= \frac{1}{2} \times 3.14 \times \frac{14}{2} \times \frac{14}{2} = 76.93 \text{ cm}^2$
Area of the shaded part $= 308 - 76.93 = 231.07 \text{ cm}^2$

16. Area of each triangle $= \frac{1}{2} \times 36 \times 30 = 540 \text{ in.}^2$
Area of 6 small triangles $= 540 + 540 - 720 = 360 \text{ in.}^2$
$360 \div 6 = 60 \text{ in.}^2$
The area of each small triangle is **60 in.²**

17. Area of the shaded part of each cube $= 600 \div 6 = 100 \text{ cm}^2$
Side of each cube $= \sqrt{100} = 10$ cm
$10 \times 10 \times 10 = 1{,}000 \text{ cm}^3$
The volume of each cube is **1,000 cm³**.

18. From 12 noon to 10 P.M., it was 10 hours.
$80 \times 10 = 800$ km
The distance was 800 km.
$10 - 2 = 8$ hr.
Calvin took 8 hr. to complete the trip.
$800 \div 8 = 100$ km/h
Calvin's speed was 100 km/h.

Time	Distance traveled by George	Distance traveled by Calvin	Difference
1 P.M.	80 km	100 km	
2 P.M.	160 km	200 km	
3 P.M.	240 km	300 km	
4 P.M.	320 km	400 km	
5 P.M.	400 km	500 km	
6 P.M.	480 km	600 km	120 km
7 P.M.	560 km	700 km	140 km
8 P.M.	640 km	800 km	160 km
9 P.M.	720 km		
10 P.M.	800 km		

$800 - 480 = 320$ km
George was **320 km** away from his destination when he was 120 km apart from Calvin.

19.
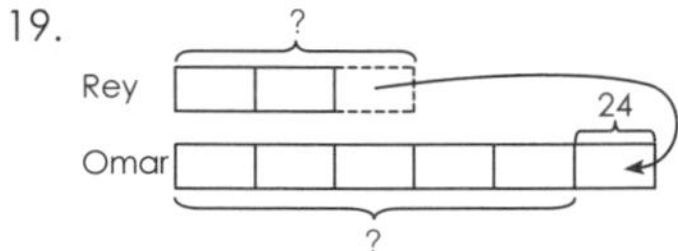

$3 \times 24 = 72$
Mike had **72** stamps in the beginning.
$5 \times 24 = 120$
Ken had **120** stamps in the beginning.

20. 12 rulers + 9 pencils $= 3 \times \$12 = \$36$
12 pens + 12 rulers $= 4 \times \$13.50 = \$54$
12 pens + 9 pencils $= 3 \times \$18 = \$54$
(12 rulers + 9 pencils) + (12 pens + 12 rulers) – (12 pens + 9 pencils)
$= \$36 + \$54 - \$54$
24 rulers $= \$36$
1 ruler $= \$36 \div 24 = \$1.50$
$(4 \times \$1.50)$ + 3 pencils $= \$12$
3 pencils $= \$12 - \$6 = \$6$
1 pencil $= \$6 \div 3 = \$2$
The cost of each pencil was **$2**.

Final Review

1. **(2)**
   multiples of 9: 9, 18, 27, (36), 45, 54, 63
   multiples of 12: 12, 24, (36), 48, 60, 72
2. **(3)**
   $\frac{45}{100} \times 9 = 4.05$
3. **(4)**
   $3x + x^2 = 3 \times 7 + 7^2$
   $= 21 + 49$
   $= 70$
4. **(2)**
   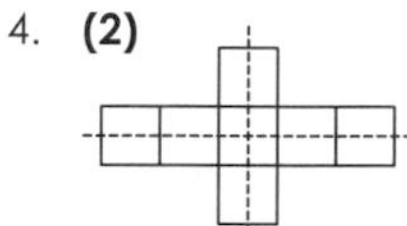
5. **(2)**
   Area of big triangle = $\frac{1}{2} \times 14 \times 12 = 84$ in.^{2}
   Area of small triangle = $\frac{1}{2} \times 6 \times 12 = 36$ in.^{2}
   Area of the shaded part $84 - 36 = 48$ in.^{2}
6. **(4)**
   $\left(\frac{w}{2} + 3\right)$ cm
7. **(2)**
   Number of rectangles in square ABCD = $4 \times 6 = 24$
   Number of rectangles needed to be shaded so that $\frac{3}{8}$ of square ABCD is shaded = $\frac{3}{8} \times 24 = 9$
   $9 - 5 = 4$
8. **(2)**
   Amount of cough medicine he took in one day
   $= 4 \times 15 = 60$ mL
   Amount of cough medicine he took in 3 days
   $= 3 \times 60 = 180$ mL
   0.25 L = $0.25 \times 1{,}000 = 250$ mL
   $250 - 180 = 70$ mL
9. **(4)**
   $5 + (5 - x) + x + x + x + x + (5 - x) + x + x + x + x + 5$
   $= 10 + 8x + (5 - x) + (5 - x)$
   $= 10 + 5 + 5 + 8x - x - x$
   $= 20 + 6x$
10. **(3)**
    A and B can be drawn as a tessellation.
    C and D cannot be drawn as a tessellation.
11. **(3)**
    $22 \times 10 \times (28 - 12) = 22 \times 10 \times 16 = 3{,}520$ cm^3
12. **(3)**
    $\frac{2\pi r}{2} = \pi r = 110$ in.
    $r = 110 \div \frac{22}{7} = 110 \times \frac{7}{22} = 35$ in.
13. **(1)**
    Height of water at first = $\frac{8{,}892}{26 \times 19} = \frac{8{,}892}{494} = 18$ cm
    $18 - 8 = 10$ cm
14. **(4)**
    Width of the rectangle = $480 \div 24 = 20$ yd.
    Circumference of the semicircle = $\frac{\pi d}{2} = \frac{3.14 \times 20}{2}$
    $= 31.4$ yd.
    $20 + 24 + 31.4 + 24 = 99.4$ yd.
15. **(4)**
    $45 \times (2 + 7) - 105 \div 5 = 45 \times 9 - 21$
    $= 405 - 21$
    $= 384$
16. **13%**
    $100\% - 24\% - 50\% = 26\%$
    $26\% \div 2 = 13\%$
17. **1,100 people**
    $24\% \rightarrow 264$
    $1\% \rightarrow 264 \div 24 = 11$
    $100\% \rightarrow 11 \times 100 = 1{,}100$
18. **42°**
    $\angle BOD = 180° - 113° = 67°$ ($\angle$s on a straight line)
    $\angle x = 180° - 67° - 71° = 42°$ (sum of $\angle$s in a $\Delta = 180°$)
19. 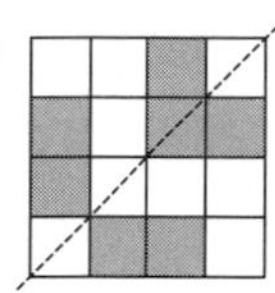
20. **$750**
    Number of cups of tea sold on Saturday
    $= 2\frac{4}{7} \times 280 = \frac{18}{7} \times 280 = 720$
    Number of cups of tea sold on both days = $280 + 720 = 1{,}000$
    $1{,}000 \times \$0.75 = \$750$
21. **14 cm**
    Volume of water in the container when it is $\frac{7}{9}$ full = $\frac{7}{9} \times 1{,}008$
    $= 784$ cm^3
    Height of water = $784 \div 56 = 14$ cm
22. **circle**
    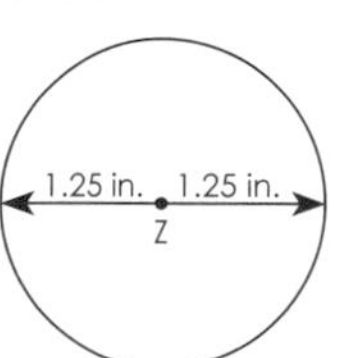

23. 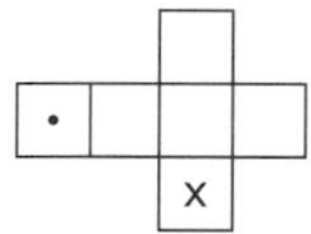

24. **140 coins**
    10¢ + 5¢ = 15¢
    A set of a dimes and a nickel is 15¢.
    $10.50 ÷ 15¢ = 1,050¢ ÷ 15¢ = 70
    Cedric has 70 sets of dimes and nickels.
    $70 \times 2 = 140$
25. **2,160 2-in. cubes**
    $24 \div 2 = 12$
    $20 \div 2 = 10$
    $36 \div 2 = 18$
    $12 \times 10 \times 18 = 2{,}160$
26. **11:14**
    Area of the square = $28 \times 28 = 784$ cm^2
    Area of the circle = $\pi r^2 = \frac{22}{7} \times \frac{28}{2} \times \frac{28}{2} = 616$ cm^2
    circle:square
    616:784
    11:14
27. **11 cubes**
    Volume of the cuboid = $4 \times 6 \times 6 = 144$ cm^3
    Volume of the cube = $2 \times 2 \times 2 = 8$ cm^3
    Number of cubes required to make the cuboid = $144 \div 8 = 18$
    $18 - 7 = 11$
28. **8.6**
29. **1 hr. 30 min.**
    From 5:45 P.M. to 6 P.M. = 15 min.

From 6 P.M. to 7 P.M. = 1 hr.
From 7 P.M. to 7:15 P.M. = 15 min.
15 min. + 1 hr. + 15 min. = 1 hr. 30 min.

30. **east**

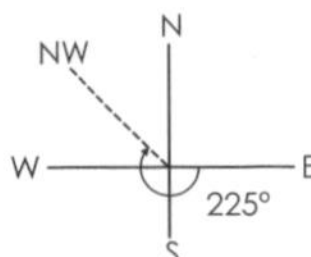

31. **3,094**
$309.4 \div 0.1 = 3,094$

32. **3.5 ft.**
$20\frac{3}{4} \div 6 = 3\frac{11}{24} = 3.45 \approx 3.5$ ft.

33. **37.5%**
$\frac{\text{Number of shaded triangles}}{\text{Total number of triangles}} = \frac{18}{48} = \frac{3}{8}$
$\frac{3}{8} \times 100\% = 37.5\%$

34. **117.3**
$230 \times 0.51 = 117.3$

35. **0.46, $\frac{16}{25}$, $\frac{23}{5}$, 6.4**
$\frac{23}{5} = 4.6$ $\frac{16}{25} = 0.64$

36. $4 - 3.187 = 0.813$ kg
The total mass of the 3 apples is 0.813 kg.
$0.813 \div 3 = 0.271$ kg
$0.271 \times 1000 = 271$ g
The average mass of the 3 apples is **271 g**.

37. $74.52 \div 23 = 3.24$ yd.
The distance between the first and the second trees is 3.24 yd.
$4 \times 3.24 = 12.96$ yd.
The distance between the fifth and the ninth trees is **12.96 yd.**

38. (a) $\angle AEB = 180° - 97° - 58° =$ **25°** (sum of $\angle$s in a Δ = 180°)
(b) $\angle ADC = 58°$ (opposite angles are equal)
$\angle DAF = 180° - 58° - 97°$
$= 25°$ ($\angle$s between two parallel lines = 180°)
$\angle AFD = 180° - 58° - 25° =$ **97°** (sum of $\angle$s in a Δ = 180°)

39. $\$(5x + 3) - \$2x = \$(3x + 3)$
A drink costs $\$(3x + 3)$.
$3 \times \$(5x + 3) + 2 \times \$(3x + 3) = \$(15x + 9) + \$(6x + 6)$
$= \$(21x + 15)$
The three boys paid $\$(21x + 15)$.
$\$(21x + 15) \div 3 = \$(7x + 5)$
Each boy paid **$\$(7x + 5)$**.

40. (a) Distance for the first two hours = R × T = 45 × 2 = 90 mi.
$\frac{3}{5} \rightarrow 90$ mi.
$\frac{1}{5} \rightarrow 90 \div 3 = 30$ mi.
$\frac{5}{5} \rightarrow 5 \times 30 = 150$ mi.
The total distance between Town X and Town Y is **150 mi.**

(b) Average rate of speed = Total distance ÷ Total time
$= 150 \div 3$
$= 50$ mph
Patrick's average rate of speed for the whole trip was **50 mph**.

41. Volume of the 6 bricks = $6 \times 12 \times 10 \times 8 = 5,760$ cm³
Water in the tank 6 bricks
720 × (9:8 → 6480:5760) × 720
The volume of water in the tank was 6,480 cm³.
$6,480 \div 20 = 324$ cm²
The base area of the tank was 324 cm².
$\sqrt{324} = 18$ cm
Its length was **18 cm**.

42. $8 \times 8 \times 8 = 512$ cm³
The volume of cube A is 512 cm³.
$728 - 512 = 216$ cm³
The volume of cube B is 216 cm³.
$\sqrt[3]{216} = 6$ cm
The edge of cube B is 6 cm.
$(8 \times 8) - (6 \times 6) = 28$ cm²
The difference between the base area of cube A and the base area of cube B is **28 cm²**.

43. (a) remaining red beads:blue beads
2 × (13:10 → 26:20) × 2
red beads:blue beads
5 × (7:4 → 35:20) × 5
35 – 26 units → 81 beads
1 unit → $81 \div 9 = 9$ beads
35 + 20 units → $55 \times 9 = 495$ beads
There were **495** beads at first.

(b) 26 – 20 units → $6 \times 9 = 54$ beads
There were **54** more red beads than blue beads in the end.

44. (a)

Category	Quantity	Charges per m³
A	First 10 m³	**$0.68**
B	Next 10 m³	$0.85
C	After 20 m³	**$1.02**

100% → $0.85
1% → $0.85 ÷ 100 = $0.0085
80% → 80 × $0.0085 = $0.68
100% → $0.68
1% → $0.68 ÷ 100 = $0.0068
150% → 150 × $0.0068 = $1.02

(b) 10 × $0.68 = $6.80
The charges for the first 10 m³ of water usage is $6.80.
10 × $0.85 = $8.50
The charges for the next 10 m³ of water usage is $8.50.
$32.64 – $6.80 – $8.50 = $17.34
$17.34 ÷ $1.02 = 17 m³
10 + 10 + 17 = 37 m³
The family used **37 m³** of water in May.

45. $\frac{1}{3} \times 210 = 70$ in.
$210 + 70 = 280$ in.
The length of the rectangle is 280 in.
$400 - 280 = 120$ in.
The base of the triangle is 120 in.
$280 \times 210 = 58,800$ in.²
The area of the rectangle is 58,800 in.²
$\frac{1}{2} \times 120 \times 210 = 12,600$ in.²
The area of the triangle is 12,600 in.²
$\frac{1}{2} \times \pi r^2 = \frac{1}{2} \times \frac{22}{7} \times \frac{210}{2} \times \frac{210}{2} = 17,325$ in.²
The area of the semicircle is 17,325 in.²
$58,800 + 12,600 - 17,325 = 54,075$ in.²
The area of the shaded portion is **54,075 in.²**.

46. $35 \times 35 = 1,225$ cm²
The area of the square is 1,225 cm².
$\frac{1}{4} \times \pi r^2 = \frac{1}{4} \times \frac{22}{7} \times 35 \times 35 = 962.5$ cm²
The area of each quadrant is 962.5 cm².

$1{,}225 - 962.5 = 262.5$ cm²
$2 \times 262.5 = 525$ cm²
The area of the shaded part is **525 cm²**.

47. 5 + 2 units → \$980
    1 unit → \$980 ÷ 7 = \$140

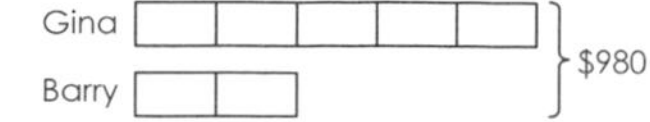

$2 \times \$140 = \$280$
Barry had \$280.
$5 \times \$140 = \$700$
Gina had \$700.
$\$280 \div 7 = 40$
$40 \times \$20 = \$800$
Barry received \$800 from his grandmother.
$\$800 + \$280 = \$1{,}080$
Barry had \$1,080 in the end.
$\frac{7}{9} \times \$1{,}080 = \$840$
Gina had \$840 in the end.
$\$840 - \$700 = \$140$
Gina received \$140 from her dad.
$\frac{\$140}{\$800} = \frac{7}{40}$
The amount of money that Gina received from her father is $\mathbf{\frac{7}{40}}$ of the amount of money Barry received from his grandmother.

48. $\frac{1}{2} \times 16 \times 18 = 144$ cm²
The area of the triangle is 144 cm².
$\frac{1}{2} \times \pi r^2 = \frac{1}{2} \times 3.14 \times \frac{24}{2} \times \frac{24}{2} = 226.08$ cm²
The area of the unshaded semicircle is 226.08 cm².
$\frac{1}{2} \times \pi r^2 = \frac{1}{2} \times 3.14 \times \frac{16}{2} \times \frac{16}{2} = 100.48$ cm²
$\frac{1}{2} \times \pi r^2 = \frac{1}{2} \times 3.14 \times \frac{18}{2} \times \frac{18}{2} = 127.17$ cm²
$100.48 + 127.17 = 227.65$ cm²
The total area of two smaller semicircles is 227.65 cm².
$226.08 - 144 = 82.08$ cm²
$227.65 - 82.08 = 145.57$ cm²
The shaded area is **145.57 cm²**.

Challenge Questions

1. $\$100 - \$85 = \$15$

$100
Betsy | Christine
Betsy | Ming
$85

Christine has \$15 more than Ming.

$81
Ming | Ming | $15

$\$81 - \$15 = \$66$
$\$66 \div 2 = \$33$
Ming has **\$33**.
$\$85 - \$33 = \$52$
Betsy has **\$52**.
$\$81 - \$33 = \$48$
Christine has **\$48**.

2. $18 - 10 = 8$
8 more people can sit around two tables when they are joined side by side.
$90 - 10 = 80$
$80 \div 8 = 10$
10 more rectangular tables are needed for 80 more people to sit around them.
$10 + 1 = 11$
11 rectangular tables are needed for 90 people to sit around.

3. Factors of 24: 1, 2, 3, 4, 6, 8, 12, 24
$4 \times 1.5 = 6$
$4 + 6 = 10$ (even number)
The two digits are 4 and 6.
Since the first digit is 1.5 times more than the second digit, the 2-digit number is **64**.

4. $25 + 21 = 46$
$46 - 13 = 33$
There are **33 children** in the group.

5. Use the Guess-and-Check method.
$14 \times 15 = 210$
$14 + 15 = 29$
The two numbers are **14** and **15**.

6. Working backward,
$4{,}455 \div 3 = 1{,}485$
1,485 tourists visited Egypt in June 2009.
$1{,}485 \div 3 = 495$
495 tourists visited Egypt in December 2009.
$495 \div 3 = 165$
165 tourists visited Egypt in June 2008.

7. Starting from the second table, 1 more person can sit around every additional table.
$100 + 2 = 102$
102 people can sit around 100 tables.

8. Based on the third hint, 60% of 5 will give a whole number, 3.

___	___	3	5
first	second	third	last

first digit = 5 − 3 = 2

2	___	3	5
first	second	third	last

$2 + 3 + 5 = 10$
$10 - 10 = 0$
second digit = 0
I am **2,035**.

9.
219
D | G
D | C
266

$266 - 219 = 47$
Carlos has 47 more stamps than Grace.

297
47 | G | G

$(297 - 47) \div 2 = 125$
Grace has **125** stamps.
$219 - 125 = 94$
Dalila has **94** stamps.
$266 - 94 = 172$
Carlos has **172** stamps.

10. $52 + 38 = 90$
$90 - 22 = 68$
There are **68** teachers in the learning center.

11.

Year	Value
1990	\$8,590
2000	4 × \$8,590 = \$34,360
2010	4 × \$34,360 = \$137,440

The watch had a value of \$137,440 in **2010**.

12. Use the Guess-and-Check method.
$16 \times 20 = 320$
$16 + 20 = 36$
Their ages are 16 and 20 years old.
$20 - 16 = 4$
The difference between their ages is **4 years**.

Notes